THE BUSINESS
OF BROTHERHOOD

V. 2.5

Thinking Strategically About Founding and Running Social Fraternities

THE BUSINESS

OF

BROTHERHOOD

V. 2.5

Thinking Strategically About Founding and Running Social Fraternities

Michael A. Smith

Created and published by

LeadOutLab
4485 Orchard Knob Lane
High Point, NC 27265

Copyright © 2011, 2012 by Michael A. Smith

Parts of this book were published earlier as *In Business for Brotherhood*.

All rights reserved. No part of this work may be reproduced or transmitted in any form or by any means, electronic or mechanical, including photocopying, recording or by an information storage and retrieval system--except by a reviewer who may quote brief passages in a review to be printed in a magazine, newspaper or on the Internet--without permission in writing from the publisher.

Michael A. Smith

The Business of Brotherhood: Thinking Strategically About Founding and Running Social Fraternities / Smith

First LeadOutLab Edition, Version 2.5– June 2012.

http://www.leadoutlab.com

ACKNOWLEDGMENTS

The ideas presented in this book have been bounced off many heads over the years.

I thank **Nat Sheppard**, **Nate Lehman** and especially **Eric Ratinoff** of Act3 Communications (http://www.thisisact3.com) for reading some truly bad early drafts and for making numerous suggestions that improved the focus and presentation.

I thank **Nathan Lux**, **Travis Ridgel** and **Charlie Trabold** for finding several typographical errors in the previous version(s). Eagle eyes!

Description of changes in version 2.5

1. A handful of typographical errors were corrected.
2. A clarifying example was included to illustrate the difference between secrecy and privacy.
3. Images were reformatted to fit better on the page.
4. The material on hazing was rearranged and some new material was added.
5. Various small wording changes were made for clarity.

Here is a special offer to readers. If you find a spelling or grammatical error in this version of *The Business of Brotherhood*, e-mail a description of it to me at **gotcha@leadoutlab.com**. If I agree and you are the first person to point it out, I will give you a shout out in the next edition.

Contents

THE BIG PICTURE 1
    A fraternity is not mysterious. Its workings are not rocket science. 2
    Fraternity chapters are essentially small not-for-profit businesses 5
    Our operating environment is changing 7
    Current challenges to the system 14
    Whom this book is for 17
AN ORGANIZATION WITH A PURPOSE AND A STRATEGY 19
    The chapter is a not-for-profit organization 19
    The chapter is a small franchise business 20
    The chapter is a niche player with a purpose 25
    The chapter is not necessarily a group of friends 33
GETTING THINGS DONE 39
    Master five basic organizational activities 39
    Measure performance. Adjust practice. 44
    Always be working toward something 49
    Practice influencing behavior 50
    Never quit running the chapter as an organization 58
FINANCES 61
    Operate above your breakeven point 61
    Manage cash like the business you are 72
    Control access to the benefits of membership 74
RECRUITING 81
    Recruit for contribution and performance 81
    Quantity is fundamental 83
    Manage the brand aggressively 86
    Be careful when bidding friends 90
DEVELOPMENT, CONTRIBUTION AND PERFORMANCE 95
    Develop to strengthen the organization 95
    Promote friendships because the chapter depends on it 97
    Be clear about expected contribution and performance 99
    Hold members accountable for their choices 102
    Don't bluff 106
    Create paths to redemption 107
    Recognize milestones appropriately 110
HAZING 113
    Nothing interesting stays secret forever 113
    The fight that is never finished 117
    Emphasize privacy instead of secrecy 122
A COMMUNITY OF STAKEHOLDERS 125
    Think of alumni and volunteers as customers 127

Become a fraternity for life 129
Empower an alumni board to help you 135
Start a chapter with an alumni association 138
Cultivate relationships with external stakeholders 139
CHANGE *145*
Plan to change something every year 145
Don't fear breaking a few eggs from time to time 146
Keep moving forward 150
Face the awkward 152
AFTERWORD *155*
APPENDICES *157*
Appendix A: Activities 159
Appendix B. Sample Dimensions of a Chapter Performance Rubric 169
Appendix C. Sample Membership Contribution and Performance Rubric 173

Figures and Tables

Figure 1. Friends and Fraternities   37
Figure 2. Basic Activity Cycle   40
Figure 3. Breakeven – A One Man Fraternity   62
Figure 4. Breakeven – Enough Members to Have Some Fun   64
Figure 5. The Sales Funnel   83
Figure 6. Devlopment and Quality   97
Figure 7. The Old Model of Fraternity   130
Figure 8. A Fraternity for Life   134

Table 1. Example Chapter Performance Rubric Items 45
Table 2. Example Membership Contribution and Performance Rubric Items
 100

THE BIG PICTURE

As an adult volunteer for my fraternity, I have made educational presentations on fraternity management for more than twenty years. Volunteers try to help chapters with almost every aspect of operations, including financial planning and record keeping, rush planning, strategic planning, how to lead a chapter retreat, and other topics. Fraternity educational programming focuses on such *operational* issues.

But volunteers also field many questions like these:

- *How do we get our members fired up to do stuff?*
- *How do we get rushees to show up at our recruiting events?*
- *How do we compete against all those chapters that have houses?*
- *How do we get more alumni support?*
- *How do you expect us to do anything when the administration is so anti-Greek?*

Unfortunately, there are no quick and easy answers to these questions because they are not about operational problems. They point to problems deeper than not having a good budgeting process or a checklist for recruiting. They are fundamental, reason-to-exist problems. If left unsolved they will eventually undermine any improvements in the day-to-day running of the chapter.

Those deep problems are the result of failing to address what businesses called *strategic* issues. To do this we must ask questions about the role the organization will play in the lives of its members and in its environment. We must think about how it will compete in the long run.

I wrote this book to help volunteers and chapter leaders identify and address those strategic issues. Along the way, I challenge many cherished notions of what a fraternity is. However, nothing I have written would surprise a business owner. It's not new; it's only new to most fraternity members. This doesn't mean that there is something wrong with the undergraduates, however.

One of the major challenges of operating a fraternity is that the membership turns over completely every five years or so. No problem ever stays solved forever in the chapter house. Each new generation must learn the same lessons. I wrote this book as an introduction to and framework for those lessons to make it easier to pass them on.

A fraternity is not mysterious. Its workings are not rocket science.

Every now and then, I hear someone say of his fraternity, *"When you are on the outside you can't understand it and when you are on the inside you can't explain it."*

That is not true.

It only seems so to members who don't yet have enough life experience to understand what a fraternity is and how it accomplishes its purposes. But to alumni who have seen more of the world and who have had time to reflect on what happened during their collegiate years, a fraternity is really a straightforward organization. Despite the legendary secrecy and rituals of fraternities, it's not hard to understand what we do and how.

Let's start with a statement about organizations in general and fill in the word *fraternity* at the appropriate place.

> **As an organization, we want our <fraternity> to be a self-sustaining virtuous cycle in service to its mission.**

At this level, we're not concerned about parties, housing, grades, athletics, participation or any of the other things that we usually strive for. Those are *means*, which are important and will be considered later.

A fraternity needs to be self-sustaining because its mission is *ongoing* unlike, for example, that of a political campaign committee. Our primary goal is to survive but we don't want just to bumble along. We want to thrive. We want to set up a feedback loop, creating *a virtuous cycle*. We want to become better and better so we can deal with changes in the environment and meet the challenges posed by our competitors.

Our virtuous cycle can be broken up into specific steps:

1. Attract and pledge new members of quality in numbers sufficient to be economically viable.

2. Foster the development of deep friendships among members. Make sure they have fun together and that they develop in ways that will help them be successful *in their own terms* after graduation.

3. Send a stream of alumni into the Big World who know that *membership in our organization* was one of the best

decisions they ever made--for the good times, the friendships and for the support for realizing their dreams.

4. Help our alumni keep in contact with their friends and develop new friendships and contacts in the organization.

5. Demonstrate to our alumni that our organization is *able and willing* to provide to new generations of members the same valuable benefits in service to a mission the alumni support.

6. Provide opportunities for our alumni to lead richer lives by giving their time, talent and treasure to better enable the organization to…

7. *Attract and pledge new members of quality in numbers sufficient to be economically viable.*

There's nothing controversial in it but it will generate a lot of questions. What is meant by *quality* and *economically viable*? Why do we even have to mention *fostering friendships?* Isn't that evident? How can we demonstrate that we are *able and willing?*

I hope to address those issues and others in this book.

Also, doubtless some folks will consider it crass to reduce what fraternities are about to a short list of bullet points.

"We're different!" I have heard. "Maximizing friendships! The Bond! That's what it's all about! We're not a business. We're a *brotherhood!*"

If that is you then before you read any further please accept for the sake of argument something that volunteers and staff members have known for a long time--*that fraternity chapters are essentially small not-for-profit businesses.*

Fraternity chapters are essentially small not-for-profit businesses

The basic challenges for not-for-profit organizations such as fraternities are the same as they are for businesses that take their profits in money: maximize revenues or services, minimize costs, and provide for survival in the long term.

When we think of businesses, we usually think of those that operate *for profit*. For-profit businesses are always under pressure to keep revenues high and costs low so they can pass the difference back to their owners. That's their *purpose*. Over the last few hundred years we have learned a lot about operating businesses to do that.

Businesses have finite resources though. They must choose carefully how to use their limited time and money to design things they think will sell. Then they have to convince people to buy them instead of spending their money on competing goods or services.

Businesses also have to do other things behind the scenes to stay in business *for the long term*, including: hiring and firing employees, developing the talent of their employees, accounting for time and money, building organizational knowledge, planning for leadership transitions, planning what to do when emergencies occur, keeping an eye out on the competition, scanning the environment for potential economic, demographic or political opportunities and threats, and keeping up with technological developments that might help them lower costs or generate revenues in new ways.

Fraternities are not businesses in the sense that software companies, athletic apparel makers, restaurants or convenience stores are. Those exist to make money. We have other purposes. Fraternities are *not-for-profit* organizations (NPOs). But, like for-profit businesses, NPOs must fulfill their purposes in a world of changing conditions, scare resources and plentiful competition.

Most people prefer not to give money to an NPO whose purpose does not interest them. They will not support an organization that they believe will waste their donation. NPOs know this, so organizations such as the Red Cross, Doctors without Borders, Girls' and Boy's Clubs, and the World Wildlife Federation work to make sure that potential donors know about the good work they do and how effective they are. And, to be effective, well-run NPOs know they must use their limited resources to generate expected profits while staying in business for the long term.

Doesn't NPO mean *not* for profit?

Yes, but when people speak of profit, they usually mean profit in *money* because *making money is the mission, the purpose, of "for-profit" businesses*. NPOs seek profits of a different kind; profits in terms of a different *kind* of mission such as vaccinating children, reducing adult illiteracy, feeding the hungry, providing after school activities for children, etc.

People who give money or time to NPOs expect the organization to maximize profit by fulfilling its service mission while keeping costs low. If they don't do these things, donors will give their money to better run organizations. Volunteers will give their time elsewhere.

Finally, few chapters run through more than $100,000 per year. They are on the small end of the business spectrum closer to a small local bakery or sandwich shop than to a high-end retailer or popular bar or restaurant.

In summary, fraternities are businesses, although not in the sense of organizations created to make money profits. Fraternities are NPOs like the Scouts, like churches, like Habitat for Humanity and every other community service or philanthropic organization that wants to continue to do its work. And individual chapters are small affairs. *Every chapter is a small not-for-profit business.*

Our operating environment is changing

The environment on campus has changed a lot in just the last ten years.

Accepting that fraternities are businesses is the first step to managing an organization well in pursuit of its mission. Next is accepting that the environment in which fraternities operate has changed a lot in recent decades. The models that served many organizations well in the past will not necessarily serve today.

For alumni, this can be a hard step to take. Many alumni want to "help" the current chapter recreate their own undergraduate fraternity experience from decades ago. It worked for them. It meant a lot to them. They believe that, if the current chapter just got back to what it was then, things would be fine. It is not hard to understand why they believe this.

Alumni returning to campus look around and see some new buildings. They see a lot of new information technology. They will likely be stunned by how much more material wealth students have than they did and how everyone walks around talking or texting on a mobile phone. But they tell themselves, "Underneath it all, it's still basically the same. Students go to class, professors are talking by their boards, there is a gym, there is a library, there is a bookstore, there are student organizations recruiting, etc. Yeah, it's still basically the same."

No, it's not. It's not the same at all.

Let me describe what college was like only a few decades ago during the *golden age* of fraternities and contrast that with today's situation.

In the late 1970s when I was thinking of going to college a co-worker in the restaurant where I had cooked pizzas since I was 16 told me, "If you go to college, go *away*. Go where you don't know anyone or you'll just end up hanging out with the people you hung out with in high school." She was one of the few people of "college age" that I knew who had really gone to college. Most of my classmates went to work full time when they graduated, many in one of the local textile mills. They married their high school sweethearts and moved into a cheap apartment until they could afford a small house or a trailer. That's just what people did. They didn't question the life path.

A year and a four-hour drive from home later, I arrived at the Georgia Institute of Technology in Atlanta. My parents and I carried my boxes and a trunk up from the sub-basement entrance of my dorm to room 444. I had some clothes, a few personal possessions, and a rolled up piece of thin yellow carpet given to me by a friend.

It was mid-September and the dorm was not air-conditioned. Fortunately, all doors opened onto the hall. Like everyone else, we opened the window right away to let the outside air pass through my room into the hall. We had to cooperate to get that cross-ventilation that was our only source of cooling.

My room had bunk beds, two wardrobes that included a three-drawer dresser in each, two chairs, and two built-in desks. The bathroom was down the hall, a gang shower, and rows of toilets and sinks that served the entire section of about fifty men.

After an hour, I kissed my mom and shook my dad's hand. They left me in my 11' x 17', concrete-walled, linoleum-floored space. The only thing I knew about my roommate-to-be was on the name card on the door: "James from Waxhaw, NC". I claimed the top bunk, a wardrobe and desk, and set my small black and white TV on the radiator under the window.[1]

The phone was a sturdy rotary-dial Bakelite AT&T standard desktop model. It was older than I was and it had a long cord so you could sit on the floor in the hall and talk if you needed to speak out of hearing of your roommate. I would rarely use the phone, however, since calling long distance was expensive, even if you used direct dial instead of going through an operator or calling collect. AT&T set the rates and you had to take them because that was *the* phone company. Since the phone was the only way to communicate long distance except for mailing letters or post cards, I wouldn't be talking with family or old friends much and never for long.

I couldn't just get in my car and drive anywhere either. First quarter freshmen didn't have cars on campus. There were plenty of seniors who didn't have cars either.

Airlines had just been deregulated but prices had not fallen yet. There were no deals or specials. Students from far away often stayed in town for Thanksgiving or went home with friends because flying home for Christmas break *and* Thanksgiving was extravagant. To buy a ticket, you had to go to the airport or a ticket office or travel agent somewhere in town or you called an airline on the phone and they would mail a ticket to you.

---

[1] I might as well have left it at home. The city had, maybe, five channels and reception was so poor in the gulch where our dorms were that watching was no fun. Besides, I soon became too busy to watch TV.

We students were on our own. Cut off from our old hometown social networks, we had to make new ones face-to-face. Students wandered through the halls. We poked our heads into rooms, introduced ourselves and started conversations. No one had to push us. Except for reading or listening to music, there was nothing to do in our rooms. The only person who seemed to know anything or anyone was the resident advisor for our section—until the fraternity guys showed up.

Late one afternoon, I sat in my room alone and bored. That was deadly for a freshman because boredom sets the stage for homesickness--a condition for which there was no electronic solution. Besides, being homesick was for wusses.

I was wondering whether to walk around campus or get something to eat at the Varsity or Junior's Grill when a shadow fell through the open doorway. Someone had walked by. Before I could get up to see who it was, a head popped around the doorjamb. In a moment, three fellows were standing there, holding beers. They stuck out their hands, introduced themselves and we started talking. They were two members and a pledge of one of the largest social fraternities on campus. They were "dorm storming" to invite people to come to rush.

I had no interest in fraternities. I had seen "Animal House". It looked like fun but I did not drink. However, when they invited me I decided right away to visit because that was better than sitting in my room, and they did seem like cool guys.

Over the next week, my life on campus opened up. During rush, I realized that I did not have to get to know people slowly by walking up to folks I happened to find myself near; There were many groups of friends *already* on campus and several of them were interested in including *me*. Sometime during the week, I decided to pledge a fraternity. In fact, I ended up with the fellows who had first asked me to come down to their house.

Years later, I was the best man of the one who had first looked into my room.

My twenty pledge brothers and I were quickly scooped up by the program. It was like going from zero to 60 in a second. We were always busy doing things together: meetings, retreats, "paddle talks" (one-on-one conversations with brothers that had nothing to do with paddling), parties, pledge weekends, house chores, and a dozen other kinds of activities that helped us get to know each other, discover common interests and learn to trust each other, and have fun.

The chapter became an essential part of our lives outside the classroom. Dorms were for sleeping and, sometimes, studying. Other times, we were out doing things and going places with each other. By the time we went through initiation, we were so much a part of the life of the Chapter and each other's lives that we could not imagine having made any other choice. In those weeks, we laid the foundations for friendships that have lasted for decades.

The fraternities of the Greek system allowed us to pool resources and coordinate activities, greatly expanding our ability to make friends and have fun. The system was the center of social life on campus. We provided most of the campus leaders. We offered alternative housing when university housing was full. We added the color to campus at Homecoming. Our organizations were the good at creating the memories that led students to become donors as alumni.

The drinking age was eighteen. It wasn't a big deal to have alcohol. Attitudes about responsibility were different. If a kid got drunk and did something stupid, as long as he did not hurt anyone, well, that is what you got for drinking too much.

Fraternities did not pay much attention to the choices of members. We were okay as long as they paid their bills and avoided burning the house down or doing something that would bring the law onto the property. The negative consequences for organizations for the bad choices of individual members usually were not great. No one had heard of liability insurance. Why would we need it?

The alumni and the national organizations practiced benign neglect, i.e. "let them figure it out for themselves". They got no argument from us undergrads about that.

Social fraternities had a ready-made recruiting pool--all freshmen males--an essential role in the social life on campus, no competition as a system, little adult oversight and few restrictions on doing anything we wanted to do for fun. The model had been successful for decades in thousands of chapters on hundreds of campuses. Golden years indeed.

Flash forward thirty years.

Because of the spread of the Internet and all the applications that use it, along with cellular telephony, the greater number of students with automobiles and lower prices for air travel, social networks are no longer limited by geography. Freshmen drag their entire high school entourages with them to college. The need to get out and meet new people face-to-face is not as pressing as it was.

Three decades ago, a student who spent all his evenings in his room would have been considered strange. These days, a student can interact with a world of friends electronically in the privacy of one of the new single person rooms. He shares a bathroom with only one other person instead of fifty and a suite with a living room and a kitchen with only three other people. If he can find a few other students from his high school, there is a good chance he will live with them. Freshmen arrive at college expecting to meet people but, even if they don't meet many, they won't be alone.

In "residence halls" built in the last few decades, bedroom doors open onto living rooms instead of directly onto the hallways. Universal air conditioning means that doors no longer have to remain open to allow cross ventilation. No longer can one just walk down the hall, lean in, and see what's going on. Today, he must knock and be invited in.

Today, drinking alcohol is a crime per se for most undergraduate students when, before, the crime was limited to other behaviors that might be associated with getting drunk such as DUI or assault or destruction of property.

Fraternities now operate under greater threat of lawsuits. As organizations that are easy to identify and who have assets, we are easy targets when tragedy occurs. School administrators are terrified of bad publicity in the age of Facebook, texting, helicopter parents and 24-hour sensation-hungry news channels. If a demonstration of the "seriousness with which we take these incidents" is legally prudent or will make a problem go away, then sanctioning an entire chapter is quicker and easier than going after individuals.

For several reasons beyond the scope of this book, there are many kids in college these days whose grades or behavior would have kept them at home a few decades ago. The pool of potential members is more variable in quality in any way you choose to measure it. Fraternities are not equipped to deal with large numbers of "kids with issues" who may pose safety and liability issues for chapters.

The rising tide of lawsuits has forced national organizations and local chapters to carry liability insurance. This cost must be passed on to collegiate members, which raises the cost of membership without raising the perceived benefits.[2] Alone, this mandatory overhead makes even a 40-man chapter shaky from a financial standpoint.

To promote retention, universities now offer longer-term housing arrangements, freshman "experiences", more amenities, more clubs, and more social programming. This raises the cost to students. Many universities borrowed money to support residence hall building binges. Now they have payments to make and see our housing as competition.

There are wider societal issues as well. Although you would not know it by looking at some fraternities, the ethnic, racial and religious profile of North America is changing. And, thirty years ago, how many kids came from fatherless households or blended families? How many openly gay members were there?

No, it is not the same environment at all.

The old model is being stressed and the system must adapt if it wants to survive. Fraternities cannot remain attached to old ways or traditions, however far back they go and however well they worked in the past. We cannot allow sentimentality and slogans to cloud our judgment or we will not be able to make the difficult choices that face us.

Current challenges to the system

In this connection-laden environment, a chapter has to offer something besides a ready-made social network to be appealing. Unfortunately many have fallen back on the most obvious thing they can provide that freshmen might have trouble getting—easy access to alcohol and the thrill of big parties. Fraternities then become (some always were) just groups of guys who like hanging

---

[2] Carrying the insurance does provide benefits but people do not join fraternities to get insurance.

out with each other and who pool their resources to put on parties and provide alcohol for their underage members.

Because of current attitudes about liability, if fraternities are to survive as organizations with assets, we must take a far greater interest in the behavior of our members. We must poke our noses into areas that, before, were regarded purely as personal matters. Things that were considered "their own business" in the past are now the concern of the organization since individual members' behaviors can and will be used against an entire chapter. It is a cloud the entire system operates under.

Fortunately, solutions to almost all the challenges fraternities face have been available for decades free for the taking in the business world. So why haven't we used that knowledge and experience to run ourselves better?

It is true that, generally, people do not join organizations, they join people. And people join fraternities for fun and friendship more than for anything else. They do not think of joining a fraternity with the same mindset with which they think of joining a gym. So isn't talking about a fraternity as a business really missing the point?

My experience has drilled a painful lesson into my head:

> **As long as the fraternity runs well as an organization, friendships will develop and flourish, but when the fraternity fails as an organization the first thing that suffers is friendship.**

I want chapters to thrive so that friendships continue to grow and members continue to have fun and develop. Fortunately, running an organization well usually comes down to nothing more than facing up to problems while they are small. When we avoid the little pain of doing that, we set ourselves up for the big pain later.

Maybe it is easier in the short run not to upset the cart, hiding behind the same old syrupy slogans about brotherhood, and hope that nothing bad happens while taking measures to insulate ourselves legally just in case. But if we are content to do that then we should not wonder why more undergraduates are not attracted to what fraternities offer and why chapters rarely reach their potential as organizations. We should quit moaning about the lack of successful and conscientious alumni to support them.

It is not a matter of business *or* brotherhood. Fraternities are in business *for* brotherhood.

And yet Greek organizations would be blind not to recognize something that sets fraternities and other NPOs apart from most businesses. Except for a few professional staff members, the collegiate leaders and the volunteers who support the work of fraternities are not in it to feed themselves. Like most people who work with NPOs, they are in it for the *mission*. They work to create a worthy purpose for their lives and to make their communities better places to live. When they run their businesses well, they accomplish their goals and they create friendships. A well run fraternity does this better than any other kind of undergraduate organization.

Despite some significant challenges, my undergraduate Greek experience was overwhelmingly positive. Like many adult volunteers, I think that the experience has been even more gratifying as an alumnus than as an undergraduate. It has also been more fun although not in ways I would have appreciated when I was younger.

In my undergraduate days, my chapter had many issues. It faced many threats. It also included some of the best and most interesting people I have ever known. Forget the stereotype of snotty dimwitted drunks from old wealth driving big cars their daddies paid for and bragging about "my beach house". Most of us took jobs to help make ends meet so few graduated on time. We arrived from all over the country, from every kind of background, and with every kind of outlook. In my chapter were young men with wonderful skills and talents, incredible intellects, noble hearts and huge ambitions.

The nearly six years I took to get out of college enriched me in ways from which I still benefit. Even years later, I rarely encounter a management issue that I did not see on a smaller scale in my chapter "back in the day". That experience gave me a tremendous leg up when facing challenges and opportunities later in life.

I believe in the mission of the organization and I want to see others derive the same benefits from membership. I also want to change the system so that more alumni choose to involve themselves in it for a lifetime.

Whom this book is for

I wrote this book for collegiate leaders and for volunteers who want to create chapters that serve their stated missions in this new campus environment. I wrote it for people who are willing to question some long-held beliefs and attitudes about social fraternities.

This is a book of ideas and suggestions, written to provoke debate and discussion and supply arguments in support of change. I wrote it to prod people to think outside the little *fratty* sandboxes fraternities have chosen to play in for decades and to encourage people to try new (to them) approaches to solving problems. I ask questions and make statements that some will consider threatening, even heretical, although nothing I propose is new to organizations in the bigger world.

I would like to see this book be a framework that undergraduate leaders and alumni volunteers with business experience can use to organize their own ideas about how more chapters can count themselves among the best businesses that have ever existed for the creation of friendships.

Now you have the background. Next we'll start the work with a statement that might seem obvious: A chapter is an organization with a purpose and a strategy.

▶

AN ORGANIZATION WITH A PURPOSE AND A STRATEGY

The chapter is a not-for-profit organization

A chapter is an organization, not its members.

To most members, the chapter is the guys they see in the room with them during a meeting. They believe that, if all of them left, the chapter would cease to exist.

But if a chapter were its members, then whenever someone left or joined, the old chapter would be gone and new one created. So what are we talking about when we say someone has *joined* a fraternity? What are they becoming part of? What is this thing that has a ritual, history and traditions independent of its current members? What is it that participates in intramurals and homecoming and Greek week? What is it that leases or owns property and whose records are filed with the government?

A chapter is not its members. It's an organization. Although we like to think of ourselves as unique because of what we try to accomplish, in terms of the challenges we face, we are more like other organizations than we are different.

We are *not-for-profit organizations*. We are 501(c)(7)s. Like other NPOs, we must address *business* problems such as marketing and sales, finance and accounting, operations management, corporate governance, human resources management, and strategic planning. It is not a matter of whether we have these issues to address. It is only a matter of whether we address them competently.

A national organization grants a charter to a local organization, giving it the right to use the national's trademarks and methods of doing business. It is an exclusive right on a particular college campus. The local may then call itself a chapter. It pays fees to the national in exchange for support in operations and marketing and product development. All locals of a given national share the same brand (usually and most obviously indicated with Greek letters). There is oversight to make sure that a chapter does not do something that would endanger the national.

In business this is called a *franchise*. Every national fraternity expands and runs itself in much the same way as any national chain restaurant or store. Chapters are franchises and their charters are *franchise agreements* with their national organizations. Each chapter-franchise is a small business locally, but it is part of a large national operation.

The chapter is a small franchise business

Chapters are small businesses and each one is a franchise of a national operation.

This is a powerful model—national standards, advertising and training combined with local money and time, and the freedom to adapt, within limits, to local environments. Every time you go out for fast food, clothes or electronics, you see evidence of the model's success. It is how businesses grow into new geographic areas and how fraternities expand to new campuses.

Thinking like a franchise operation, we run into our first problem with most fraternities. Consider why and how chapters are founded compared to how a well-run business would sign a franchise agreement with and support a local operation.

Fraternities should create only interest groups and colonies that will strengthen the national organization.

The best run businesses do not allow a franchise to open just anywhere a local businessperson wants to give it a shot. Headquarters has an idea of what kind of environment they operate successfully in and they gather information about areas for potential expansion. Expansions are allowed only where they are likely to succeed and therefore to *enhance the strength of the national operation.*

Unfortunately, national Greek organizations are generally not so careful about expansion. If there is a local group that is "fired up to be XXs" and the college administration is agreeable, then the interest group is formed. The demographics of the school, the means of the typical undergraduates, the availability of high quality local volunteers, the educational standards of the institution and the likelihood that a chapter there will generate alumni who are able and willing to complete the circle by supporting the undergraduate organization are not always taken into account.

Interest groups and colonies should only be planted where they are likely quickly to add value to the national organization in terms of reputation, finances, and the generation of successful, active alumni. If a new group is not doing these things, what is it to the national operation but a drain on resources and a source of likely future problems? How can headquarters justify to its other chapters/franchisees the use of scarce resources to support that group?

> **Local constitutions, by-laws, policies, and procedures should be fill-in-the-blank documents.**

Successful national operations do not grant franchise agreements and then sit back while the local owner develops all his own policies and procedures for running the business. They train the new owners and monitor the progress of the operation. Although they encourage involvement in the local community, they do not allow the owner to do just anything he wants regardless of the effect on the brand. The local franchise must operate within some limits. We should do the same with interest groups and colonies.

However, despite the fact that almost nothing about running a chapter is unique to a local situation, it is normal to allow each colony to write its own constitution and by-laws. Under a misguided notion of creating "ownership" of the local group, we allow people who have no experience running a chapter to create their own policies and procedures for most areas of operations. This reinvention of the wheel wastes time and distracts the new organization from what it really should be focusing on, which is deciding what it will be on that campus and then growing quickly into that role.

Each chapter must be accountable to the national organization and to each other chapter for how it represents the national brand on its campus.

After chartering, we generally hold our local chapters much less accountable for standards and behavior than a national restaurant chain hold its franchisees. We would do better to insist, however.

When a chapter of your fraternity loses a lawsuit anywhere, you have to cough up higher liability insurance payments. Indeed, fraternities pay dearly for liability insurance, in great part due to bad choices made over the years by of a bunch of guys you have never met and have probably never even heard of. You don't just pay financially though.

Scenario

You find yourself across town at lunchtime and see a sandwich shop you have not tried before. Curious, you go in.

- *Scenario A: The menu has little on it that interests you. The service is slow. They get your order wrong. The cashier is one of those who doesn't seem to know how to work the register even though it has pictures on the buttons instead of numbers. He acts as if his confusion were your fault for ordering no tomatoes on your sandwich. There is a tip jar on the counter that reads, "Dear Customer, Tipping is not a city in China." When you unwrap the sandwich, you see they put tomatoes on it and then took them off.*

- *Scenario B: The menu has a couple of sandwiches on it that look interesting. The maker verifies that you don't want tomato and asks whether you'd like to substitute something else for it. Your order is completely quickly and correctly. The cashier has it rung up for you before you even get to the register. The sandwich tastes great.*

In which scenario are you likely to tell all your friends about the sandwich shop? A few months later, another franchise of the same sandwich shop opens right in your own neighborhood! In which scenario do you believe you will probably try it?

Think of the worst chapter of any fraternity on your campus. Imagine that chapter representing *you* on another campus where the brother, sister, girlfriend or parents of a guy you are rushing interacts with them. What do you think that will do to your chances of recruiting that prospect even though you have no relationship at all, beyond those letters, with that other chapter? He might have written you off before you have a chance to show him what you're like. You probably do not even know those people in the other chapter but they have taken something from you. They have reduced the value of the brand you are tied to. They have made it more difficult for you to operate. Who in the world did those guys think *they* were to do that to *you*?

Think about what it could mean to you as a graduate. You might be a valuable member of a well-run chapter with tons of experience that would make you the perfect choice for a position. But what if the recruiter did her undergraduate work at a college where your fraternity's chapter was a bunch of jerks or slackers? What if she *personally* had a bad experience in the house that displayed your letters? If she doesn't understand how different chapters of the same fraternity can be, that's likely to affect her perception of you although you had nothing to do with her experience. Again, who in the world did those guys think *they* were to do that to *you*?

In summary, in the Greek world, not only are we on the hook for each other in terms of liability but the conduct of a chapter on one campus will definitely affect the ability of other chapters of that fraternity to recruit through the impression of the national organization it creates. It may even affect how potential employers look at your members.

The chapter is a niche player with a purpose

> **A good market niche contains enough potential members to allow the chapter to be selective in recruiting while meeting its recruiting goals.**

In the larger world, a business must make its product or service unique in the eyes of its customers so they have a reason to choose it over the competition. If the product is, more or less, identical to that offered by competitors, the product is called a *commodity*. Businesses that sell commodities usually compete on price or by hoping that they get to the customers before the competitors do.

Low price usually means low margin[3]. Small businesses should avoid competing on price because they must sell a lot just to generate enough cash to survive. Price competition is generally left to "Big Box" retailers who make profits because they sell so many of each thing they stock.

Normally, it is best for a small business to find a market niche based on having a product that is *different and superior* in a way that is important to some pool of potential customers while performing acceptably in other areas. This is what a chapter must do on its campus.

---

[3] The difference between what one of something costs you and what you can sell it for. If t-shirts cost you $12 each and you sell them for $13.50 each, the margin is $1.50 per shirt.

The majority fallacy or "the hamburger trap"

Find groups of sharp potential members that existing chapters do *not* serve and figure out how to create something useful to them.

So you want to start a restaurant? It should be easy because there are already so many successful restaurants out there. Just pick one that is doing well, do what they do, and you will succeed, right?

What will you make? Why not hamburgers? Look at how many hamburgers those fast food restaurants sell. Don't most restaurants offer hamburgers? What more proof do you need? It is obvious that hamburgers are very popular so let us make some and use a successful competitor as our model. Only we'll be *cheaper* than they are so people will want to come to our place instead. Yeah, that's the path to success. Come on! Let's grab a piece of the action!

When starting a new business, it is tempting to identify what "most people" or "the typical consumers" want and create a product or service to provide that. That would mean more potential customers, right? Sure, except that that is exactly the group that most of the other people who are starting and running businesses are going after as well. This is such a common strategic error that there is a name for it in business: *The Majority Fallacy*. It is a hard place to stay for any business, which is why competition among national restaurant and soft drink brands is so fierce. It is a death trap for startups.

Good luck competing against those well-run, well-known operations and, by the way, notice that even the big burger chains don't offer just burgers. And most restaurants that do offer burgers offer a whole lot more, including a different atmosphere.

To succeed, you must do something different from what others are doing.

Red Ocean / Blue Ocean

Offer something existing organizations cannot or will not offer. Dodge around their strengths and run your own race.

Colonies and small chapters are tempted to model themselves on the successful chapters around them or on stereotypes of fraternities they have seen on TV or at the movies. They take what seems to work and try to duplicate it. But that means taking on existing chapters in areas in which they are already strong.

You would not do this if you were opening a new restaurant or store, however. If there were already five pizza restaurants on the street, you wouldn't open just another pizza restaurant. *Instead, you would offer something competitors could not or would not offer.* You would build your strength where they are weak.

A new chapter that seeks to compete in the same recruiting pool as a group of existing organizations is following a "*Red Ocean*" strategy[4], so called because the water is full of the blood of competitors. The challenger will be a small fish in that big red ocean.

The alternative is differentiation that appeals to the *unmet* needs of a large enough pool of potential members who are not interested in what existing competitors offer. This is called a "*Blue Ocean*" strategy. This is not really competition; the challenger does

---

[4] Kim, W. C. & Mauborgne R. (2005). *Blue Ocean Strategy*. Boston: Harvard Business School Press.

not challenge. It does not even run the same race. It picks another race to run and goes for victory on its own terms.

Bases for a niche

> **Instead of thrashing around in the Red Ocean, your chapter could increase the offering of the entire Greek system by appealing to people that are not attracted to existing organizations.**

You can always find something that your competitors do not consider important enough to spend time or money on. There is some combination of characteristics that can set you apart from all the others: academics, athletics, community service, ethnicity, demographics of your members, housing, field of study, level of dues, support for ambitions, connections for internships, attitudes about "traditional" fraternities, attitudes about current social issues, religion/philosophy, hobbies, etc.

Alternatively, one could pick a niche based on not being exclusive in some ways that other groups are. Reputation is also a characteristic, one whose value is often overlooked.

Occupying a new niche strengthens the system without hurting existing organizations. You will face little competition because you do not threaten existing interests. Your chapter can focus on making members of the untapped pool aware of the new offering instead of trying to use its meager resources to measure up to existing organizations.

Promoting your chapter in a niche market is easier and less expensive than promoting in the mass (everyone) market. Your potential members are easier to identify and to design and deliver targeted marketing material to. Think of how the Marines advertise, for example. They know what their niche is and they put the word out in a way specifically designed to attract the people they are looking for in just the places those people are likely to be looking at.

By the way, one advantage that new chapters may have over older ones is *agility*. A new chapter can pick its characteristics more easily and can change directions faster than older ones who may have reputations, commitments to facilities, powerful internal politics, and unreasonable alumni expectations–*baggage*.

In any case, finding a way to stand out from the competition–that market niche–and then figuring out how to dominate other campus organizations in that niche is a logical strategy for a chapter. That means figuring out how to become the *first choice* of people in your recruiting pool even if it means changing the organization in ways that would have turned away existing members when they were freshmen. It means finding a niche the chapter can thrive in even if some of the alumni drift, or stomp, off.

Remember, before you can pass the chapter on, you must have somebody to pass it on to.

One natural niche for fraternities

The only thing a student could do that would be more instructive in business than helping run a large social fraternity is to start his own enterprise.

A well-run Greek organization already occupies a niche that is ready-made for us on campus. We are small businesses that deal with most of the problems businesses in the larger world face. Leadership, management, budgeting, accounts payable and receivable, marketing, event planning, continuity planning, discipline, strategy, liability, facilities maintenance, education—a well-run Greek organization deals with all these things. So do badly run Greek organizations; they just deal with them badly, which can be a good source of lessons as well.

Learning how organizations thrive long term in the face of competition and changing conditions is a tremendous potential benefit to membership. Why not become good at that and promote it?

The niche is described in the mission

Dwight D. Eisenhower[5] once said "Plans are nothing; Planning is everything." So it is with missions. A mission statement is the "talk that guides the walk".

Great organizations think about what they are trying to accomplish, about why they exist. That reason guides their actions. A common tool for clarifying an organization's purpose is the *mission statement*.

All chapters have missions. Most of them are unwritten and unspoken but can be figured out easily simply by looking at what the members do. Unfortunately, many missions are not attractive propositions for alumni volunteers, university administrators, faculty members, law enforcement personnel, or parents of prospective members. This is one of the causes of the Greek system's difficulties with these groups.

Before your eyes glaze over thinking about your big serious mission statement, step back and think about what it amounts to. It's only a short statement of what your chapter is about. Think

---

[5] Allied Supreme Commander in Europe during WWII and 34th president of the United States.

of the mission statement as an *elevator pitch*. An elevator pitch is an overview of an idea, product, or service designed to be told to somebody in a short time such as while riding an elevator. Elevator pitches are common in business, where they may be used to weed out poorly thought out or off-target ideas quickly.

Keep it short. The entire mission statement should fit on *one page* in a type size that is readable (11-12 point size at the smallest.) If you can't fit it on one page, either you are trying to do too much or you are going into too much detail about what you do.

A mission statement has two parts. The first explains *why* the organization exists—its *purpose*. This is likely to be generic since most fraternities are founded for the same reasons.

Each of the points should begin with a verb in the present tense. The entire set of points fits together as a (long) sentence but something that could easily be transferred to a website or any promotional material. For example:

We have organized the AAA chapter of BBB fraternity at CCC in order to:
- *support the academic success of our members,*
- *develop our members' personal effectiveness, social and leadership skills,*
- *have fun,*
- *foster a network of lifelong friends and colleagues.*

The meat is in the second part of the mission statement. This is where the organization begins to differentiate. Here in broad terms, the organization specifies *how* it accomplishes its purpose; its chosen *means*. Each of these should relate back to one or more of the points in the purpose and each point of the purpose should match to at least one point in the means section. Each of these points should begin with an *-ing* verb, which implies action.

As with the purpose, the entire set of points fits together as a (long) sentence. For example:

We accomplish these purposes by:
- *aiding new members to develop behaviors and skills that lead to academic success,*
- *requiring older members to demonstrate academic effectiveness,*
- *providing experiences to develop the leadership skills, moral and ethical sense and social aptitude of our members,*
- *creating social events and activities for our members and their friends,*
- *partnering, as a group, with other campus and community organizations,*
- *promoting mutually beneficial interaction among undergraduates and alumni and*
- *acting to sustain our organization.*

It would also be useful to have a statement at the end such as "We expect each member to support this mission. We enforce individual conduct standards to that end" since this sets the stage for some important practices we will consider later.

Mission and niche are related and both should be determined at the same time. This can be exciting and it can be uncomfortable. It may expose differences between why the organization claims to exist and why it really exists. Nevertheless, it is important because the mission provides a common document that all stakeholders can refer to when deciding what the organization should be doing. It will also help in figuring out how well it is doing and where it needs to improve.

As competitive conditions change, the mission statement changes as well, but this should be done only with a lot of thought, which leads to the next point.

The Board should keep the mission

The undergraduates and the Board should review the chapter's mission and niche from time to time to make sure they remain appropriate for the environment on campus.

Board involvement is essential because that group is best placed to bring a long-term big-picture perspective. As well, a chapter whose mission is not supported by a group of talented alumni will find itself on the ropes and friendless eventually. The chapter will bumble from crisis to crisis, issue to issue, always reacting, and rarely taking on challenges that require long-term thinking. Eventually it will screw something up badly and have to endure a house-cleaning or shut down. Do you know some chapters like that?

On the other hand, a chapter with an attractive mission that it makes an honest attempt to fulfill will have something it can use to approach alumni volunteers, university administrators, and parents. That opens the doors to a flow of benefits from stakeholders in the wider world.

The chapter is not necessarily a group of friends

A chapter is not necessarily a group of friends. A chapter is an organization that *promotes* friendships, among other things.

Many chapters begin as circles of friends, founded with the intention of imitating existing groups. Regardless of what they say about being different, their plans are, more or less, "become just like everybody else except it's me and my friends instead of them and their friends." Different doesn't mean different ends or means to them. It just means different people.

A group that exists only to provide a sense of belonging and cool t-shirts for a group of friends is not a fraternity. To survive, the organization must quickly expand beyond pre-existing friendships because, no matter how much the guys like themselves as a group, if there are not enough of them to make financial sense (which we'll get to later), they're probably better off not being a fraternity.

If a chapter is based only on the liking the members have for each other, rush/recruiting becomes an attempt to find people that like the members. A small chapter is not a good base from which to try to expand a circle of friends unless each of the members is extremely active and well thought of on campus.

Friendship is a goal, not necessarily a starting point

Fraternities must create environments in which friendships can form and grow.

Fraternities are not mystical organizations that can create friendships overnight through exotic rituals practiced on groups of students from whatever background, with whatever interests. Relationships form and work within human limits. There is a limit to the number of true friendships a person can have, if friendship is more than being "Facebook friends".

During one of the soul-searching five-hour meetings that my chapter had during my undergraduate days, a member spoke out against a proposal to establish some modest membership standards concerning grades, participation, and finances. He was frustrated that we had forgotten what seemed to be an obvious truth to him.

"A fraternity is just a group of friends," he said. "That's all we are—*a big group of friends.*"

He argued that people who were trying to make more of it were missing the whole purpose of the organization. It was easy to see his point since one of the dozens of little things we memorized as pledges was that the purpose of the fraternity was *to maximize friendships.*

In fact, most of my friends at college were among my fraternity brothers. It was no accident. I had known no other students when I arrived. After pledging, I was surrounded by people who wanted to get to know me. Friendships developed though the things we did together, some fun, some not, as members of the fraternity. The fraternity provided the means for us to become friends, fulfilling its stated purpose of maximizing friendships.

However, I do not believe anyone in our large chapter would have claimed that every other member was a friend of his. In reality, each of us had six to ten others that we spent most of our time with. With the rest of the members, we were good company and helped each other but there simply was not enough time to hang out with everyone like we did with our friends. We were *fraternity brothers*; we were not as close as friends but we were closer than to other students and closer than we had been to many of our friends in high school.

Under different circumstances, *any* of us might have become friends. In fact, as our circumstances changed during our collegiate years and after graduation, old friendships faded and new ones formed with others in the chapter. It was good being in a large chapter because it gave each of us a large pool of potential friends. In the meantime, we got along well with a lot of people and that enriched all of our lives.

There were also people in the chapter who did not like each other. That might sound strange, given the idea of "brotherhood" but, if you gather enough people from different backgrounds and keep them together for long enough in an environment in which there are consequences for people's actions, eventually, some of them will not get along. If they did not have to cooperate for the Good of the Fraternity, they probably would never have had much to do with each other.

Fortunately, any lack of friendship rarely became obvious since, unless he habitually disrespects you, it is hard to dislike someone deeply who is washing dishes or cleaning the house with you, or working as hard as you are at a chapter service project or playing his heart out on one of your intramural teams, and who comes to chapter meetings and pays his bills on time, however little you enjoy hanging out with each other.

Friends or not, we all wanted our fraternity to be a fun place, to win in athletics and campus events, to be admired, to be big, to have enough money to throw great parties, to have lots of girls around, to be full of people we liked, to be a place where we felt comfortable and proud. We were all willing to work toward those things, toward *The Good of the Fraternity*. Although we disagreed sometimes on the details of what that Good was and on the means for attaining it, we were bound by our dedication to the welfare of the chapter. We worked together for the sake of an organization for maximizing friendships--but not necessarily our friendships with each other!

Figure 1 illustrates the reality of friendship and fraternity. You probably are on good terms with many people. Some of them will be in your fraternity. Some of the members will become your friends if your organization is fulfilling its purpose, but not necessarily all of them. Most of your chapter will consist of guys you get along with although you are not as close to them as you are to your friends. And, yes, there will be a few members that you don't like much, especially if your chapter is large.

Figure 1. Friends and Fraternities

Although, it would be great if you could point to each member of your chapter and say "there is a friend of mine", in an organization that is large enough to make sense financially (explained later), it will probably not be so. Acting as if it must be makes us too selective for the wrong reasons during recruitment and not selective enough when it comes to holding people accountable for their behavior as members.

Now that we have a better idea of what a chapter really is and isn't, let's consider how a chapter delivers on its promises.

▶

GETTING THINGS DONE

Master five basic organizational activities

You are helping lead an organization whose undergraduate membership turns over completely each four or five years and that relies on volunteers for long-term support and continuity. But those volunteers cannot run the day-to-day operations of the chapter. Undergraduate members will always be in the front line everyday doing the things that make the chapter work. If it is going to run smoothly, those undergraduates need to know how to do their jobs correctly.

> **For the sake of continuity, you must teach members how to run the chapter.**

Learning how organizations thrive in the long term in the face of competition and a changing environment is good preparation for life and your chapter could be a great place to pick up skills most people don't come across until well into their twenties, if ever.

A basic activity cycle is a good way to think about the things that have to be done right to ensure that the organization survives. The cycle includes five activities that your chapter must master to be a good organization. These activities will support everything else you do. They are illustrated in Figure 2.

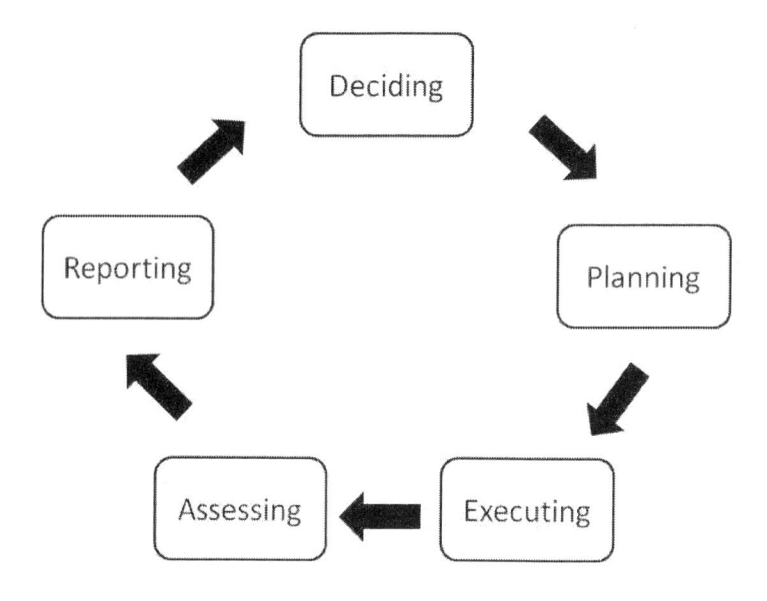

Figure 2. Basic Activity Cycle

The basic activities are:

- **Deciding**: There are always more desires and choices than there is time, money and people. How are decisions made? Who gets to decide? What's the purpose of the activity? What are the measurable objectives? Did you ever wonder why Robert's Rules of Order[6] have been used for so long?
- **Planning:** Big projects need to be broken down into smaller ones. What roles need to be played? Will training be necessary? What resources are required to get something

---

[6] http://www.robertsrules.com/

done—people, money and time? When are they needed? How are we going to get them? How will we know when we have accomplished our purpose—can we create some milestones?

- **Executing:** Once we kick this thing off, how are we going to coordinate the use of all the resources? How are we going to monitor progress? Communicate? Make mid-course corrections to keep on track? Let everyone know how we're progressing?
- **Assessing:** Conduct an "after action review". How did we do compared to our objectives? What went well? What could we do better next time? Overall, was this worth the resources we expended?
- **Reporting:** Let's get credit for the things we accomplished with the school and the fraternity. Otherwise, how will they know? How will prospective members know? The alumni? Let's make a record of what we did so that the next group that comes along (maybe us again) can benefit from our experience when they are making decisions, planning, executing, etc. In the wider world, assessing and reporting are essential to continuous improvement.

Resources the chapter has

Your chapter has six kinds of resources to use to accomplish each of the five activities. Three of them are part of the individual members and three of the organization. Making sure that you have these resources and use them well is a key to running the chapter well.

The individual resources are:

- **Hands a.k.a. manpower:** "Many hands make light work." When you are organizing a fundraising event, helping with freshman move in, having older members tutor younger ones, making a space for the chapter in other campus organizations, doing the bookkeeping, planning events, dealing with the dean, or doing anything else that requires that a human being take action, manpower is an issue. Do you have enough? Do your recruiting practices guarantee an unending stream of new members? Do you have the systems in place to be able to call upon the membership and organize the use of it? If enough manpower is not present in your organization, can you partner with another organization to get enough?

- **Money:** Not everything a chapter does requires money but you have to lay out money for insurance and national and IFC dues and fees before you can operate as an official organization. And, once that's done, much of what chapters traditionally organize themselves for (parties, for example) requires funding. So do you have enough money? Do you have systems in place to predict what you'll need, make sure you get it, keep track of it and report how it was used? If enough money is not present in your organization, can you partner with another group to share the cost?

- **Individual abilities:** Sometimes you just need hands to show up for the work. But sometimes you need the heads to show up as well. Do you have the skills and talents in your membership to plan and execute the activities you undertake? Do you have programs in your organization for developing the skills and talents of your members so that the chapter always has people ready to step up to run things well? How about recruiting with specific skills and talents in mind? (This might sound strange but it has been done for decades—think of chapters that have a history of dominance in particular sports, for example.)

The organizational resources are:

- **Meetings:** This is where everything that needs to be handled with the membership *in the same place at the same time* is done. A lot of *deciding* is done in chapter meetings. A lot of *planning* is done in chapter, committee and ad hoc meetings. Some *executing* may happen in meetings, for example conducting membership reviews. Groups may meet to take stock of recent results and *assess*. Meeting outcomes are habitually recorded and *reported*.

    Meetings are also important for a chapter for *social* reasons. It is impossible to understate the importance of this social aspect of meetings especially in a large chapter or one that does not own a house. Weekly chapter meetings might be the one time and place where the entire membership sits down together. This is where all members are reminded by the company of others and the routine of ritual and order of business that they are part of something that is bigger than they are. This is where members may interact *as fraternity brothers* with members that their housing arrangements and schedules rarely permit them to see—a powerful reminder of what it means to be part of the fraternity, something that will only grow more meaningful as time and distance separate them after graduation.

- **Communications systems:** A good organization has ways to inform and to coordinate the work of its members when they are *not all in the same place at the same time*. E-mail, text messaging, phone, website, bulletin boards, etc.—The chapter must have a program for using tools to communicate and, just as important, all members must be tied into the system and know how to use it. How often are they expected to check e-mail? Does the chapter have a way to distinguish its official emails from others so members can pick them out quickly? Is there a system in place for making sure all members can update their contact information easily and that the other members can get that information when it's updated?

- **Organizational knowledge and skills**: In the end, all of an organization's power to accomplish anything resides in the abilities and willingness of its members to take action. That said, that ability and willingness can be greatly enhanced if the chapter has structures for gathering information, using it, storing it and passing it on. If the chapter is in the habit of doing these things, it will create a great base of organizational knowledge and skills that will give the chapter an alternative to "reinventing the wheel" or "making it up as you go along". This will save a lot of time and money and greatly reduce the frustration of members.

Measure performance. Adjust practice.

All fraternities have declarations of purpose or principles that they present to recruits and to new members. They are all beautiful thoughts worded beautifully. They are usually presented as "something we try to live up to". How much more powerful they would be if, when they were read out, they were followed with "and we do live up to them. Here's how."

Great organizations rate their performance against goals regularly in order to celebrate when they've met their goals and make changes when they haven't. This is a serious process, deserving thought about how measurements are done, and time to evaluate the chapter at the end of each term. However, it does not have to be difficult or time-consuming.

A *rubric* is simply a way to classify things. You can create one to classify your chapter's performance in ways that relate to its mission. If you do this well, using the rubric later will be quick and painless.

Create a chapter performance rubric

A rubric is easily represented in a grid with three columns. In the first column are the dimensions of performance that will be measured. Each dimension that you are measuring occupies a row. These dimensions relate to the items in the means part of your mission statement. It is not necessary to measure everything but it is desirable to measure the most important things.

The remaining two columns include criteria for classifying performance: satisfactory and superior. To receive a mark of "superior" on a dimension, the chapter must already have satisfied the requirements for "satisfactory" on that dimension. Not meeting the satisfactory level implies "needs improvement".

Dimension	Satisfactory	Superior
Aiding new members to develop behaviors and skills that lead to academic success	• All candidates demonstrate proficiency in note-taking, time management and study skills as a condition of initiation	• Chapter enforces a minimum GPA standard above good standing for initiation.
Requiring older members to demonstrate effectiveness	• Chapter enforces a minimum GPA standard for continuing membership.	• Each candidate and member contributes at least one standard course notes file to the Chapter library each term.

Table 1. Example Chapter Performance Rubric Items

Qualifications for classifying your chapter on a given dimension should be clear. Each measurement should be specific and easy to make. If it's not, people will quickly tire of it and quit. It does not have to be perfect, however. An adequate measure that can be made easily 100% of the time is better than a perfect measure that can be made 80% of the time or with difficulty. Examples of chapter performance rubric items are presented in Appendix A. Table 1 shows an example for two dimensions from the mission given earlier. Creating measurements should be a cooperative effort of the undergraduates and the board. And keep in mind that satisfactory is a *minimum* standard. What the chapter is striving to be falls under superior.

In this example, the chapter must decide how candidates will demonstrate proficiency and what a standard course notes file looks like. After that, it's just checking off boxes.

Not only is a rubric useful for helping your chapter improve itself but it can be used to show stakeholders and prospects that your mission is more than just "something we try to live up to". A completed rubric is great framework for strategic planning meetings, meetings with boards and advisers, and year-in-review sessions. *What matters and how are we doing? Well, let's have a look…*

Rate the chapter's performance

It is possible to attach a label to the chapter based on its performance against the rubric. For example, assume the chapter evaluated itself on 10 dimensions.

- **Marginal**: More than eight ratings less than "satisfactory". Chapter functions as a "group of friends" but is no "band of brothers" (as depicted in the mini-series of the same name.)
- **Existing**: No more than four marks less than "satisfactory". Chapter is probably not in immediate danger but its long term survival and thriving is questionable.
- **Satisfactory**: No mark less than "satisfactory". Chapter does no harm to the brand, is involved in its community and is likely to thrive in the long run. There is a sense of

purpose and improvement. Chapter can be selective in membership and is definitely a positive influence on the lives of its members—it functions as a "band of brothers".

- **Superior**: No mark less than "satisfactory". At least four marks of "superior". These guys have their act together. The chapter is an asset to the brand through its conduct and activities. It is important to the community and can be highly selective in membership.
- **Exemplary**: No mark less than "satisfactory". At least eight marks of "superior". Chapter is well known, universally respected and is considered an essential part of its community. To be a member is considered a sure indication of current and future success. There is a sense of excellence.

This way of measuring chapter performance resembles the *balanced scorecard approach*[7], which has been around for decades. This approach recognizes that there are several ways of looking at an organization's performance, each of which should be monitored. The classic dimensions are: financial, customer, internal process, and learning and growth. It's not a big stretch to see how the things we do in a fraternity could be classified using those dimensions.

What do you do with the classification?

The chapter and its board can use the rubric in *any way they choose*. For some, the rubric will be useful as a framework for discussion

---

[7] Kaplan R S and Norton D P (1992) "The balanced scorecard: measures that drive performance", *Harvard Business Review*, Jan – Feb pp. 71–80. The technique has been refined since it was introduced and managers now speak of second and third generation BSC documents.

during periodic reviews and strategy sessions. *What specific areas of operations do we need to improve on?*

Other chapters and boards might attach some organizational consequences to chapter performance. For example:

- **Marginal**: Changes in operations and/or membership required to continue. Large-scale board or HQ intervention should be expected.
- **Existing**: Board or HQ intervention is likely on specific dimensions.
- **Satisfactory**: No specific action indicated.
- **Superior**: Chapter will be pointed out on its campus and to others in the fraternity as an excellent source of ideas for improvement.
- **Exemplary**: Chapter will likely be asked to serve as a "brother chapter" to a colony or struggling organization. Chapter may be eligible for reductions in per member HQ dues and fees.

In any case, a chapter performance rubric is a crucial link in the chain that connects the organizational mission to the behaviors of individual members. Just as the dimensions of the rubric measure the chapter's performance against its stated purpose and means, *Membership Contribution and Performance rubrics* can be created that link individual behavior to supporting the measures in the chapter rubric. That is the definition of quality in the context of membership. It is an essential and powerful connection since all organizational behaviors and characteristics flow from the choices of individual members.

Always be working toward something

Get busy living or get busy dying.

Groups never maintain their current level. They are either rising or falling. If it looks like nothing is happening, the group is probably slowly falling. You must be working at something.

In the motion picture *The Shawshank Redemption*, Andy Dufresne never gives up the hope of regaining his freedom. However, he does not just hope, he works at it. With a tiny rock hammer, he takes years to dig his escape tunnel, giving meaning to a life that might otherwise have been wasted languishing and enabling him to endure the setbacks and indignities of prison life. Founding the library, running the tax preparation service, and even playing an excerpt from the opera *The Marriage of Figaro* on the public address system—all of the projects he took on enlarged his life and the lives of everyone around him. It is the same for an organization, like your chapter, that has a noble purpose, goals and resources.

A chapter must always have goals and be working toward them. For a new group, the goal is the charter, then perhaps its first championship or recognition on campus or by the national organization. New groups typically need to grow. Eventually most look for a house to call their own. Later they make work to establish a scholarship endowment or a mentoring program or to furnish or refurbish the house. There is always *something* else that the chapter can strive for and it is important that such a goal always be in front of the membership.

These goals should not be arbitrary. They must be taken on because they clearly will improve the organization in ways that all the members can understand and buy into with their hearts. Those are goals people can live for.

Inspiration follows perspiration.

The most difficult part of taking on something new is taking the first step. Winston Churchill[8], who painted watercolors as a hobby, was intimidated at first by the blank canvas. He remarked that early in his practice he was dabbing around with a tiny brush when a friend grabbed a big brush, swabbed a big chunk of color and laid it on the canvas, thus removing the intimidation.

How do you begin a new lifting routine at the gym? You start small and get a partner to hold you accountable and to spot for you. It's the same with every new venture. Plan small first steps and get everybody in it together. Think of ways to make it fun.

And, when a goal is reached, don't succumb to the temptation to "take a breather". Set the next goal. It doesn't have to be a bigger one. It doesn't have to be difficult. It simply must be a step in the right direction in the long term for the chapter.

Practice influencing behavior

People behave in accord with their own interests—as they perceive them.

Although you may cherish the differences among members, no fraternity's principles imply that anything goes. Your chapter has a strong interest in influencing the behavior of its members and of others in ways that benefit the organization. Most members have never been part of anything like what you are. You must educate and, yes, *indoctrinate* them so that they will know what

---

[8] Prime minister of the UK during World War II who overcame a terrible childhood stammer to become one of the great public speakers of the 20th century. This was mentioned briefly in the motion picture "The King's Speech" in which the king of the UK had to overcome the same handicap.

they must do to support the chapter. Learning how to get people to do what you want to them to do is essential to your success and is good training for organizational leadership both during and after graduation.

When I was an undergraduate, my chapter had problems in many areas of operations including grades, finances, and involvement. So I appointed several committees and assigned them specific deliverables describing what the chapter would do to address these issues. They took their charges seriously and proposed some good programs and standards in all areas, to be put in place by some by-law changes. For example, there was to be an internal social probation if your grade point average got too low and there were to be mandatory tutoring hours. After a lot of wailing in chapter, all the by-laws were passed. Then nothing. Zilch. No improvements at all. We had all spun our wheels for weeks designing these wonderful policies and procedures without asking ourselves for a second whether we though anyone would actually abide by them and enforce them. We thought we had accomplished something. After all, the by-laws were so well thought out. But we had accomplished nothing but having wasted a lot of time, unless you count the life lessons learned. We had not done anything to address the reasons for which members behaved as they did. We had not given anyone reasons to change their behavior. So nothing changed.

Anyone can pass a by-law but why do you expect officers to enforce them if they only represent an idea of what would be good instead of what the members are really willing to support? We pass by-laws that we like to think of ourselves living up to but, when the consequences come, often we back away from the pain of enforcement. Then we wonder why people do not respect the by-laws or the authority of officers.

A person who is running an organization can avoid a lot of frustration and heartache by recognizing some things about human nature. People do not behave necessarily as they promised or in accord with the by-laws or as you wish them to behave. They behave in accord with their interests. Save yourself a lot of trouble and give up expecting otherwise. For example, if a chapter's by-laws state that bills are due in full at the beginning of the term but the chapter routinely allows people to wait until the end of the term to pay without penalty while offering no rewards for paying at the beginning, a lot of people will wait until the end of the term to pay.

You get what you recognize and incentivize. This is the key to getting people to do what you want them to do. If you keep this in mind, understanding much strange behavior and motivating people to be helpful becomes a matter of figuring out what people really want as opposed to what they say they want.

Different people are motivated by different things but all people seek pleasure and avoid pain.[9] If you want to know what really brings them pleasure, look at what things, people, and situations they repeatedly gather to themselves through their choices. If you want to see what causes them pain, consider the things their choices indicate they are avoiding.

Develop a boxful of motivational tools

People seek pleasure and avoid pain—as they perceive them.

When thinking of how to motivate people, leaders and managers must have a toolbox of options that includes rewards and punishments (carrots and sticks) that the chapter is able and

---

[9] This is simple most of the time but it gets interesting when a person finds pain in something most find a pleasure in or finds pleasure in something most people consider a pain. That topic is *definitely* beyond the scope of this work.

willing to dole out and that are strong enough to motivate members. Although some people are self-motivating, others will require some prodding to raise the importance of issues in their consciousness.

Reward, also known as positive reinforcement, is an after-the-fact pleasurable consequence of an action. "If you do what I want, I will give you something you want." For example, if you want people to pay their bills in full on the first day of classes, offer a discount for doing that. That is a reward for the desired behavior.

One of the easiest ways to create rewards is to look for opportunities to make things *fun*. Almost anything can be made fun by making a game out of it, introducing some competition, letting people work with their friends, and getting together after with the other participants to celebrate.

I worked in a Pizza Hut when I was in high school. The pay was low, the hours were long, the kitchen was hot, sometimes the customers were jerks, and there were always many dishes to be washed by hand. Yet overall, I enjoyed it there because I was friends with most of the other employees and we made a game out of the work. From the moment the shift began, the practical jokes, smart-aleck comments, and competition to see who could work faster began as well. After closing on Friday and Saturday nights, we put slugs in the jukebox, cranked it up and played the game of seeing how fast we could all finish cleanup together. Then we'd all go to the 24-hour Denny's down the street and unwind until close to sunrise. It was hard work and it wasn't fun every second. (It wasn't fun when I found out that it was not a floral pattern on the seat of that high chair, for example.) However, we made it fun by how we approached the work.

This is not strange. This approach has been used for millennia by people to make difficult or boring work bearable.

Consider the scene in "Cool Hand Luke" when the prisoners are cutting grass by the road. Think of the end of "Seven Samurai" when the villagers are planting their rice crop. In Celtic music, there is a tradition of call-and-response songs for "waulking" cloth that to modern ears are rhythmical and beautiful but that are in origin work songs. Sea chanteys and the songs of the gandy dancers are also work songs used to coordinate tasks and pass the time.

This is not a call to go out and make up work songs, though you could do worse. The point is that the technique of making an experience rewarding by making it fun is nothing new.

Negative reinforcement is an unpleasant sensation administered to encourage the desired behavior. "I am putting pain on you and, when you do what I want, I will take the pain away." For example, members may not vote or attend parties until they have paid their bills—they are effectively excluded from chapter activities. This is the pain. However, once a member pays up, the restrictions are lifted *immediately* and they can take part in everything.

Punishment is an after-the-fact unpleasant consequence of an action. "You did something that displeased me therefore I will put pain on you and there is nothing you can do now to stop it." For example, "you missed a payment deadline and I am tacking a late fee onto your bill. Don't bother arguing about it."

Generally, rewards are more effective than negative reinforcement and punishment is the least effective. But people are different. Some people's reward threshold is so high that the organization cannot afford to offer them an incentive. On the other hand, some people will exhibit a desired behavior simply for recognition. Still others will do it because they see that it conforms to their own interests (whatever they believe them to be.)

As well, people find different things painful. Simple shame or the loss of some coveted privilege such as voting, housing or participation works for some people. A fine system will motivate some people but may not be motivating to members who are not accountable to their parents for the money they spend. They will just opt out of the desired behavior and let their parents pay the fine. In this case, clearly you would have to think of something else to motivate those members.

For a given incentive, certainty is as important as degree

When it comes to consequences, certainty is as important as severity.

There are two aspects of every consequence: how desirable or undesirable the consequence is and how likely the consequence is to occur. Both are crucial.

To make a chapter work, you must first make desirable the consequences of individual actions that are in the chapter's interest and undesirable the consequences of actions that work against the chapter's interest.

Outcomes must also be certain in order to be effective motivators. For example, the most undesirable consequence, expulsion from the membership, is rendered ineffective as a motivator if everyone knows you will never follow through on the threat. On the other hand, a relatively small fine or loss of privilege, if certain, will eventually influence the behavior of members.

People are more likely to do what they believe they can succeed at

Most people will avoid doing things at which they doubt their ability to succeed if their failure will make them look bad. So if you sense that kind of reluctance around an action, educate and train the members. For example, if you want them to use an on-line dues payment system, sit down with them the first time to show them how to do it and make sure they know they can call you for help if they need it later.

If people are reluctant to undertake some task because they doubt they will finish in time, break the task up into smaller tasks. In all things, identify the skills, knowledge, and tools people need to do the job and make sure they have them. *Empower them*. That is good management.

People are influenced by what they regard as normal behavior, i.e. the "culture" of the organization

When you pledged, how did you learn how members behave in each of the many situations in which you found yourself? You probably learned a few things from listening to your educator tell you things. Maybe you asked a few questions. But, mostly, you just kept your eyes and ears open. You learned by watching others. Sometimes they were careful to show you the right way to act but, most of the time, they didn't know you were watching or they didn't care. All of your pledge brothers learned in the same way. Some even watched you and noted how others reacted to things you did. All of the existing members learned as you did, by watching older members. Each group of pledges that came in after you watched you and the other members.

You have a constitution and by-laws but you also have something even more powerful for influencing behavior—*an organizational culture* a.k.a. a set of social norms. "It's what we do" is a powerful motivator, especially for younger members who are still seeking acceptance in the group.

In all things they do or say, older members model acceptable behavior for candidates and new members. Discuss this openly with older members and confront any who maintain that they didn't sign on to be a model. There is no opting out. They are examples whether they would like to be or not.

This influence is a two-edged sword. It can make good members but the presence of blatant slackers whose behavior is obviously accepted presents a model of membership contrary to the chapter's interest. Especially when members label some work "pledge work", that impression sticks in candidates' minds and they will be reluctant to do it after initiation. If public drunkenness is praised, they will regard it as desirable behavior. If members are always telling candidates "don't worry about grades", the organizational culture will come to ignore academics. If members habitually trash the facilities and leave the clean up for work parties later, the message is that you do not have to pick up after yourself.

So what does your culture look like? What behaviors are your older members modeling for the younger ones?

The buck stops with the leadership

Chapter leaders can sit back and complain that members "ought to" do this and do that but, in the end, if they are not doing what the chapter needs them to do, the leadership has simply failed to create the right set of incentives. Words are not effective in the end. Like a new year's resolution, they will soon be forgotten unless something else changes, something in the underlying expectations of outcomes, organizational culture, or ability to be effective. If the chapter leadership cannot or will not address those underlying factors, there is little hope of managing an organization or of causing needed change. In that case, alumni advisers, who have fewer limits on their power and who are more distant emotionally, may need to step in and make some fundamental changes to the organization.

Never quit running the chapter as an organization

When in the jungle, always dress up for dinner. The deeper the jungle, the better the dress.

When an organization is new, small or having problems, it is tempting to set aside things like regular meetings, ritual, and agendas. "We run things kinda informally here" is a phrase I've heard used to excuse this although it explains nothing and it justifies nothing. It simply means "We're not serious."

If you are new or small, you are especially vulnerable to degenerating into mere groups of friends. You should give the most attention therefore to the practices that clearly indicate that your chapter is more. Your members need to remind themselves often that they are part of an organization with a mission.

The author Anthony Burgess, who wrote *A Clockwork Orange* among other things, remarked about the British practice of dressing up for dinner especially in remote regions far from visible signs of their culture:

"[The British] regard dress and deportment as an aspect to action. If they did not dress for dinner in the jungle, they would just wear the same clothes they were wearing all day long ... They would relax. Everything would relax. Law would relax. Discipline would relax. The jungle would creep back again. So

they deliberately did this. It was not foolishness. It was a deliberate technique for maintaining self-discipline."[10]

From day one as a colony, you must take care to conduct yourselves as an organization and to master organizational competencies. This is more important than fraternity history or learning the Greek alphabet.

- Hold chapter meetings at the same time and place each week so that it becomes part of members' schedules.[11]
- Conduct ritual regularly if you've been trained. If it's done correctly, it probably won't add more than fifteen minutes to the meeting and it is a reminder that the chapter has greater purposes.
- Use a standard order during each meeting. This is the framework for the agenda into which the officers insert specific items to be taken up at a given meeting. This adds to the "professional" atmosphere and helps keep meetings from dragging out.

No matter the situation, maintain the organizational structure and practices that are described by your by-laws, policies, procedures and rituals.

In the next chapter, we'll look at one of the primary reasons for which chapters fail—lack of money. Not surprisingly, this will be both the cause and effect of another problem—lack of members.

---

[10] From Bunting, C. (Winter 1973) "An Interview in New York with Anthony Burgess". *Studies in the Novel.* v.5. n.4. North Texas State University.

[11] Our chapter always met on Wednesday nights. *For years after I graduated,* I habitually avoided scheduling anything for Wednesday nights.

FINANCES

Operate above your breakeven point

The only thing one can say about most small chapters is that they are too small and too poor to do much worth joining for--which helps them stay small and poor.

In the late 1990s, as the resident advisor of my chapter, I watched our uphill neighbors across the street during their annual fall quarter pre-rush workweek. All week they struggled to repair the awning over their front door, a project that would have taken just half a dozen of our members a morning to finish, because we had the manpower, the tools and the skills to tackle jobs like that ... and at least a dozen other such jobs during workweek.

Size brings with it access to the resources that you need to do what people join fraternities for. If you are too small, you won't be able to do much. If the best you can do for a social event is to pass the hat and (illegally) buy a few cases of some bad beer and some bags of chips, what is the point? You don't need to be a fraternity to have activities at that level.

How big does your chapter need to be? That depends on your overhead costs, your ambitions, and how much your members are willing to pay. There is no single number that works for all chapters but there is a process that will give you a good number for your chapter.

Figuring out the breakeven point

Consider the case of a one-man chapter, if such a thing could exist. To keep things simple, say he pays $100 total each term for membership.

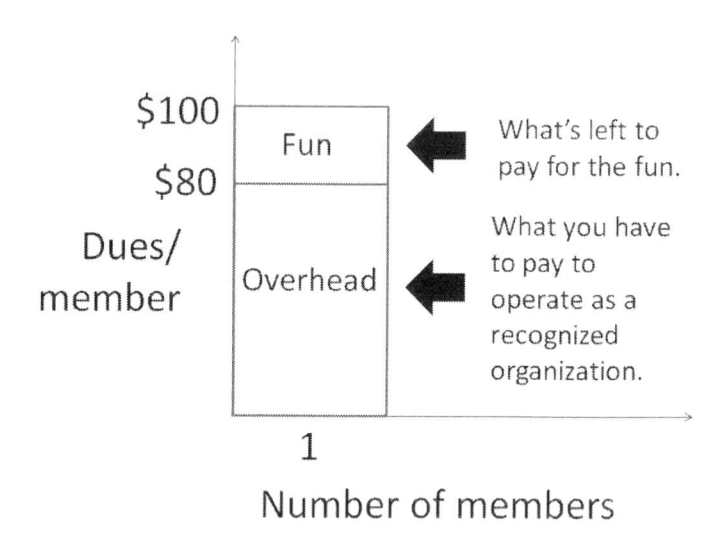

Figure 3. Breakeven – A One Man Fraternity

From that $100, the chapter (he) has to pay the national organization and the IFC dues and liability insurance. These add up to $80. That is his overhead cost of being an organization. There are important benefits to having national affiliation, insurance and school recognition. However, those are not why people join fraternities. That leaves the one-man fraternity $20 with which to do those things that he created his chapter for. He's paying $100 for what benefits $20 can provide. Obviously, that makes no sense. He'd be better off not creating a fraternity and, instead spending his $100 on a good time for himself. This strange situation is depicted in Figure 3.

Since his 1-man fraternity makes no sense, he gets two friends to join. (This might seem strange but it's exactly what a lot of small chapters try to do to survive.) Each of them pays $100, of which $80 goes to overhead. That leaves $60 among the three of them to have some fun with. That is still not a good deal.

Having five members paying $100 each still generates only $100 total for benefits *if* the group can agree on something(s) to do that would provide $100 in benefit in the mind of each member.

Somehow these guys avoid folding and, after a major recruiting drive, the organization has fifteen members! Now they're up to $300 dollars total to spend when each member is only in for $100. This situation is depicted in Figure 4.

Economically, the scales have tipped but there is still a problem. The leader has to find something(s) to do for $300 dollars that will seem like a good deal *to each member*. And what kinds of things can you really do for $300 that everyone can and will participate in? Why not, instead, dump the chapter and have $1,500 with which to do some things? After all, there are only fifteen members. That's not difficult to coordinate.

Even if they raised the dues and fees to something more realistic--say $350 per term for dues and $210 per term for fees-- the situation does not change. It costs money to do many of the things for which people join fraternities. Unless the chapter is clearing enough money after all the overhead has been paid, it won't be able to provide an attractive combination of those things. The chapter is heading for trouble and its members are going to be recruiting prospects into a bad deal.

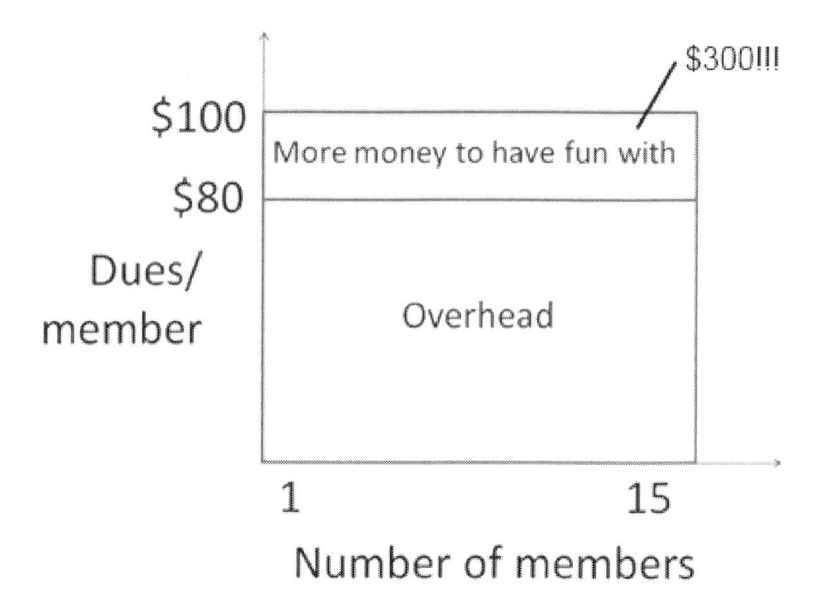

```
                                              $300!!!
                                             /
 $100 ┌─────────────────────────────────────┤
      │   More money to have fun with       │
 $80  ├─────────────────────────────────────┤
Dues/ │                                     │
member│              Overhead               │
      │                                     │
      └─────────────────────────────────────┼──→
      1                                    15
              Number of members
```

Figure 4. Breakeven – Enough Members to Have Some Fun

Say this to a fifteen-man chapter, however, and they will insist that their brotherhood is "tight" and that they are all about quality, not quantity.

How realistic is that though, really? How can a fifteen-man chapter compete in intramurals and in Greek Week and homecoming? How can they throw parties that many people would want to come to? How likely is a new member to find an older member in his major who can help him? If just one member out of fifteen pulls a GPA in "the square root club"[12], what effect will that have on the chapter GPA compared to the effect it would have on the grades of a seventy-man chapter? If the chapter needed someone with a specific skill or knowledge, which would be more likely to have such a member, a chapter of seventy or one of fifteen?

There are chapters of all national organizations that fool themselves into believing that there is something virtuous about being a very small organization. They claim that the quality of brotherhood is better. It's a bunch of bull. No matter the chapter size, a person will still have only so many close friends. In a big chapter, you just have more choices.

There is nothing good about small.

So how big does a chapter need to be? It's easy to figure out with three figures:

- **Total overhead costs** – One big number that includes everything that is passed through to the IFC, a national organization, the insurance company, etc. Basically, this is stuff members have to pay just to be recognized as an organization. This is a total amount, not per member because, usually, you get one big bill each from HQ, the IFC and the insurance company. So just add it all up.
- **Total fun money** needed to do the things the members joined to do, as well as covering things such as officers' expenses.
- **Maximum dues per member that you are willing to charge.** This must include *everything that is mandatory* for a member to pay. If a member pays this amount at the

---

[12] When the square root of your GPA is higher than your GPA. Do the math and figure it out.

beginning of the term, he's good for the term as far as the fraternity is concerned.

Then do these simple calculations:

- Add total overhead costs and total fun money, giving total expenses.
- Divide total expenses by maximum dues per member. Add 10% to that number to cover people that don't pay their bills and you have how big the chapter needs to be.

For example, if your chapter needed to cover $8,000 in overhead costs and had social ambitions that would require an additional $10,000, you'd need $18,000. To hold dues to $350/member per term, you would need to have fifty-two members. With 10% to be safe, it comes to fifty-seven members. If you wanted to be safe, add 15% or 20%. That's all there is to it.

You should use this number to set goals for recruiting in the coming year. How many new members do you need to replace graduates and grow or stay at the membership level you need? This is a *meaningful* recruiting goal, superior to the "last year plus some percent" method, because there is a *consequence* for not meeting the goal--dues must go up or fun money must be reduced.

Meaningful goals are powerful. Think about how much easier it would be to motivate members if you could translate their actions or inactions into consequences as easy to understand as those of recruiting results. You might even present alternative budgets to the chapter based on how many new members you get. Finally, consider how convenient for members and parents it is to take your dues as set rather than having them vary widely from term to term as many chapters do.

Vicious and virtuous cycles

If your chapter dropped below the membership needed to provide the benefits it wanted to provide, it could decrease benefits, increase dues or run up debts to pass on to the next generation. Each would start the chapter on the path downward.

If you decreased benefits, then the remaining members would receive less than they thought they would for what they paid.

If you raised dues, you might price the organization beyond what some members were able and willing to pay even for the benefits.

The last option, passing on debts to future generations, is just wrong unless those future members will get some direct benefit from the expense. For example, maybe your chapter buys bandstands that will last for five years. Unfortunately, however, most expenses passed on are for things consumed by the current generation.

No matter what, the pressure on membership will be downward. That is the beginning of the death spiral, the vicious cycle. As membership shrinks, the work of supporting your chapter financially and otherwise falls on fewer members. In the end, who will be left holding the bag? Maybe the wealthiest members who did not care about money but, more likely, the ones left will be the most loyal members, those who struggled to find ways to keep paying their bills and who sacrificed to support the chapter. That's the group that most deserves to be *rewarded*, not punished.

How would you feel about recruiting new members into an organization that did not make financial sense? How would you feel about recruiting to pay off old debts? Imagine making this pitch to a potential member: *"Hey, I know we have nothing to offer you as a member that you can't do more cheaply for yourself without the obligations of membership but, frankly, we really need your money so that this makes sense for those of us who are already in it. So won't you please join and, by the way, we've got this big debt we need your help paying off as well..."*

On the other hand, as the number of members grows, since overhead expenses are covered, the amount of discretionary spending can also grow. Eventually the benefits that can be provided may become large enough to support greater dues because members perceive the greater benefits as worth paying more for. This is the virtuous cycle.

To be sure, as dues increase, the potential pool of members decreases *unless* you can provide some new benefits that increase the size of the pool of prospects. But as long as your chapter can recruit enough members, okay.

However, there may be a strategic reason for not raising dues even if you could. Charging lower dues than the market would support for the benefits provided should allow your chapter to be more selective during recruiting and more demanding of existing members. That is a good situation to be in.

In summary, when costs are greater than perceived benefits, you are operating in and recruiting new members into a losing proposition. Basically, you have to trick or charm recruits into joining by lying about costs or exaggerating the benefits. On the other hand, when perceived benefits for each member are greater than the costs, inviting new members to join your chapter truly is offering them a gift.

Final points about breaking even

These points apply especially to colonies and small chapters, as you would expect. However, every one of them also applies to large chapters.

- ***A colony must reach breakeven quickly.*** A colony must *quickly* reach the breakeven point for providing the benefits that people join fraternities to gain. An organization that starts as a circle of friends and expands slowly by meeting other people casually is likely to perish. For a colony, the number one priority is *growth*. Put the brand out there, recruit aggressively and get over the breakeven point. Then quickly implement a development program that promotes the growth of friendships among all those new members.
- ***KISS.*** (Keep it simple, stupid) If your chapter keeps things simple and cheap in terms of benefits, it is possible to get along with fewer members than if the members choose to use the chapter as a vehicle to advance grandiose party ambitions.
- ***Beware overhead.*** If you are small, committing to a lot of organizational overhead is risky. A dip in membership because of graduation, grades, or other reasons can suddenly cut the fun money substantially, tipping the balance against membership. Or you can raise dues. However, this would decrease the size of the pool of potential members at the very time when you need to be more attractive to increase membership.
- ***Leverage campus and stakeholder resources.*** Especially for small chapters, leveraging good relations with the administration, other campus organizations, or other chapters, or alumni can make the fun money go farther. If you are small, find ways to provide benefits that do not depend on money by using things that students are paying for through student activity fees. That will help level the playing field because most organizations do not even think in terms of leverage. For example, can personnel from student life provide educational programming or facilitate brotherhood activities? Can you work with with other campus organizations for outdoor activities and community service? Are there educational or social events occurring on the

campus that can just be included in your chapter's schedule? Instead of throwing your own parties, could you just coordinate mass attendance of your members at a campus party? Instead of hiring your own bands, could you buy a block of tickets to a local venue that his hosting a popular band? Will an alumnus let you hold a retreat at his house?

- ***Remember the 20/60/20 rule.*** In any chapter, count on about 20% of the people always showing up when something has to be done. Another 20% will never show up. The remaining 60% will follow whichever group seems to be having the most fun at the time. Well, for getting things done, 20% of seventy gives you fourteen people, which is better than 20% of twenty, which gives you four. This is another reason to grow quickly and stay large.
- ***Small chapters live just one bad rush from disaster.*** Your chapter needs to be able to withstand some downturns. Consider a minimum chapter size of forty-five for that reason even if you could breakeven at a lower number. At forty-five, you have the manpower to survive a year of recruiting failure without plunging into the vicious cycle. You will have a chance to regroup, evaluate and respond.
- ***Each year, hold a financial planning session.*** It should cover:
    o Budgeting ahead for a year based on what it will cost to provide the benefits its members want to have.
    o Coming to a consensus regarding the target bill. Keep in mind that raising the bill generally cuts down on the size of the recruiting pool while putting the bill too low will hurt the organization's ability to deliver benefits that will attract new members.
    o Finding out how many members will likely be lost in the coming year due to graduation, transfer, quitting, etc.
    o Determining what your break-even point on membership is, given the desired budget and bill.

- Setting the recruiting goals that support the chapter's plans.

Make the results of the planning session available to every member and his parents and to the alumni. Everyone should know exactly how the bill was decided and why the recruiting goal is what it is. This is part of what businesses call *transparency* and it is a good way to build confidence in the leadership of the organization.

- **Create the expectation that a successful recruiting year is one that puts your chapter at or above its breakeven point.** There is no other measure of success in recruiting. There is no "quality vs. quantity" argument to be made. Recruiting is a success if you get enough new members to enable your chapter to carry out its plans. Otherwise, recruiting was a failure. However, it does not have to be an epic fail if your members think about what happened and why and change your chapter's recruiting practices to do better next time.
- **Count on some loss of members, aka "attrition",** for several reasons: grades, money, transfers, loss of interest, etc. It always happens but high attrition is a waste. It is a loss of the time and money you invested in recruiting. Now you must devote even more resources to recruiting to replace the members you lost. A high attrition rate may be an indicator of several things including:
  - Failure to be up front with recruits about requirements, especially financial and grade requirements.
  - Failure to provide high value experiences to upperclassmen as well as to underclassmen.
  - Recruiting the wrong kind of people—people who are not dedicated to the organization but only to hanging out with their friends.

If you suffer high attrition then you must be extra good at recruiting. But think of what your chapter would be if it were good at recruiting and had low attrition!

Now, assuming that you have a handle on financial planning, all you have to do is manage the cash.

Manage cash like the business you are

Assuming that your chapter is big enough, the thing most likely to stand between it and doing all the things it wants to do that require money is cash flow. Fortunately, solutions are not rocket science.

Collect what is owed you

Fraternities may offer easy terms but we do not offer free anything. Fraternities take on financial obligations on behalf of their members, enabling them to pool their money to do things that they could not do by themselves. We depend, however, on everyone chipping in his share as determined by the fraternity.

So what about people, even initiates, who are the very embodiment of everything we stand for as an organization except that they simply cannot afford to pay?

The world is full of such people. To avoid the heartbreak of having to deal with them as members we must be up-front about *all* costs and expectations when they are recruits and candidates. We must also be clear that membership is not the same as friendship. And we must conduct ourselves professionally when we are billing and collecting from them:

- *Use an on-line receivables service.* Your chapter must keep records of every billing and every receipt so that a member or his parents can understand his balance at any time. A service will do this. As well, it will make it easy for

members and parents to get up-to-date information and pay in several convenient ways. A service will also automate discounts and penalties.
- Members must be billed consistently in a way that they expect – post, e-mail, note under the door, etc. Whatever it is, members must be reminded that they have been billed and told whom to contact if they did not receive a bill or if they have questions.
- Members and parents should know where the money is going. The chapter must provide a copy of the budget with the bill and upon request.
- Payment terms must be clear, along with incentives and penalties.
- Special arrangements must be put in writing with signatures. Writing things down helps avoid honest misunderstandings among friends. It also gives you something to point to if the member reneges on the promise to pay.
- Failure to pay must lead, in the end, to a collection agency. No one should be able to walk away from a bill. It sets a bad precedent and leads to cash flow problems later. The chapter can be patient. As long as the member is making payments and staying in communication, it is good to work with him. But if he stops paying and starts avoiding calls and messages, you have to close the loop without him. A receivables service will help you with this.

Control and monitor spending

If an officer can make himself look good simply by spending more money, eventually someone in that office will do it. Many experienced treasurers will tell you that their most important duties are keeping the checkbook balanced and saying "no" to the guy who plans the parties.

Access to the chapter checkbook or card must be limited to a handful of people. They must be trained to keep receipts so that anyone could come back later and satisfy himself that chapter funds were being spent appropriately.

Speaking of appropriate spending, don't even try to buy alcohol with chapter funds. There is no shell game that has not been run, no strange reimbursement scheme or rolling of alcohol into other expenses that will slip past a dean, a staffer from headquarters or an experienced alumni volunteer. There is nothing new under the sun when it comes to hiding this—only things that are new to the current group of undergraduates. And what signal does this send to members, especially new members, about the kind of organization you are? What are you if you routinely lie to the alumni volunteers that support you, to the administrators of the campus that hosts you, and to the national organization that has granted you a franchise, putting the time and money they have invested in the organization on the line-- over your desire to use chapter funds to pay for alcohol?

Watch that cash flow. The treasurer must keep records up-do-date so that he knows at all times how much cash the chapter has. Officers often believe that, because their budgets include a certain amount of money, they are authorized therefore to spend that money whenever they need to as long as they don't go over their budget. If the chapter collects all its dues at the beginning of the term, this will work. However, most chapters do not, so officers need to clear expenditures with the treasurer to make sure the checkbook does not go negative.

Control access to the benefits of membership

To survive, your chapter must offer a set of benefits that members and potential members

see as worth giving up time and money for *and* that the chapter can and will control access to.

Generally, people avoid paying for what they can get free. In fact, if they don't have to pay for a thing, they will take it even if they want it only a little. Witness the success of on-line music file sharing in the early 2000s and the creation of collections of MP3 files by college students despite the financial pain their actions inflicted on the very artists they most preferred. It did not seem to matter than one could not hope to listen to 10,000 songs either.

Along those lines, if different organizations offered nearly identical benefits, people would probably go with the one that cost them less. Otherwise, they would have parted with more of that scarce resource (money) that they could have used for other things. That runs against their interests.

It's the same with time. If people can choose to contribute time or not to in exchange for a benefit, most will take the benefit and find other uses for their time. Again, they probably see it as against their interests to do otherwise.

On the other hand, if the benefit is worth the cost, most people will pay if that is the only way they can get the benefit. There are two parts to this idea.

- The value of the benefit is worth the cost.
- The only way to get the benefit is to pay for it (membership).

If either of these conditions is not true, then most people will not pay. They will take it without paying for it or they will choose to do without it. In fraternity terms, they will show up for the fun stuff but will not support the organization by paying dues and giving time or they will not join because they do not see the benefits as worth the costs.

To be successful in the long run, you must offer benefits that you *can* and *will* deny to non-members.

No membership "à la carte"

Membership is membership. Stay away from special statuses based on individual situations.

A senior in a chapter I was advising decided that he wanted to move out of the chapter house for his last year and into an apartment off campus. Not only that, he was taking a newly initiated member with him.[13] The chapter had a large house that had to be kept nearly full for its financial model to work so they had had instituted a "parlor fee" that ensured that living in the house would always be cheaper than living off campus *as a member*.

So the treasurer said to him, "Fine, here's the out-of-house brother fee."

"If I have to pay that," the senior replied, "I won't be able to afford to pay rent for my apartment. But I might be willing to chip in this amount," He mentioned a much lower fee, "to help pay for parties and such. Take it or leave it."

Several members took the view that some money was better than nothing so the chapter should accommodate the guy and make him a "social affiliate." That would have been a mistake, however, since there were other members who worked hard to

---

[13] The senior had been the candidate educator the year before. The kid he was taking with him had never even lived in the house but the senior needed a roommate to be able to afford to live in the apartment he had selected.

pay their dues and rent. If they let this fellow dictate his own terms of membership, why not those guys? What would the chapter do when a member presented himself, with a tear in his eyes and a sigh in his voice, claiming that family problems meant that he could no longer afford to pay full rent but he might be willing to pay *some* if he could still live in the house?

Life situations change. The financial and time resources of initiates change. Sometimes a fellow doesn't have enough to do all the things he'd like to. But he would like to avoid having to choose. Hey, what if he could persuade someone who has a claim on his money or time to give part of that up? Whom could he ask?

- The bank that holds the title to his car? *No, they'll send the repo man for his car and invite a reality TV show to film the action.*
- The cell phone company? *No, they'll drop his service, but at least he won't embarrass himself anymore with his texts from last night.*
- The university he must pay tuition to? *No, they'll just drop his schedule and refuse to supply a copy of his transcript until he clears up his library and parking fines.*
- The landlord that owns the apartment he lives in? *No, they'll evict him, send some thugs to set his stuff on the curb, and then take him to small claims court.*
- The fraternity? *Heyyyyyyyyy .... They're all his brothers aren't they?*

> **Never ask in the name of brotherhood. Only give in the name of brotherhood. Better still, just give and let others see the brotherhood in your actions.**

We have a phrase to describe people that we like and that embody everything we stand for as organizations but who cannot or will not pay the dues and give the time necessary to sustain the organization. We call them "guys we like who are not members".

It feels good in the short run to choose to spend other members' dues subsidizing housing or social costs for members who aren't paying. The guys who aren't paying are grateful because you behaved in such a "brotherly" manner and they will shower you with praise and thanks. This should not surprise you since they've got their hands in your back pocket. If you push them away, they'll have to make some decisions they'd rather not make.

But, in letting things slide, you are setting yourself up to have to pass judgment on a stream of individual situations later. And it does *not* feel good to choose *not* to spend other members' dues as subsidies when the person who wanted the help is standing in front of you, upset, asking why you won't do for him in the name of brotherhood what you did for others.

To avoid having to call initiates out, chapters create special exceptions, such as "inactive" or "social affiliate" statuses that enable them to skip around the reality of the situation. This is a misguided effort to practice *price discrimination*.

Price discrimination is a valid method for increasing income in some industries by creating classes of products or services that will appeal to groups who are not able or willing to pay full price. The business enlarges the pool of potential customers by creating *market segments*. For example, movie theaters set different prices for children, students, and for senior citizens. They also set different prices for matinees.

However, they can practice price discrimination *only* because they alone decide what the classes are and who belongs to them. For example, the student cannot decide on his own to take the student discount. He must demonstrate to the ticket seller that he should belong to that class and the ticker seller, not the student, makes the decision.

Such price discrimination *might* work in a chapter if it kept for itself the right to decide who could be such an affiliate and how the application could be made. It *might* work if the chapter agreed that no individual member could opt out of fulfilling responsibilities to the organization by unilaterally declaring himself "inactive". Then the issue would be whether a chapter would say "no" to one of their own who sincerely believed that his hardship case justified "inactive" status. The only thing an individual member could do without the chapter's consent is resign.

As well, to make a "social affiliate" status work, your chapter must be able and willing to control admissions to events. That is difficult since even people who have renounced membership have friends in the chapter who will want to see them at parties. If other friends of members can come, why exclude entrance to friends who are former members? What if the event is at a member's house or apartment and he wants to let the person in?

Finally, excluding such former members is a thankless task for an officer. Does he really want to spend his evening arguing with members or trying to catch them violating guest book policies?

Here are some suggestions for when a member insists that he cannot pay and asks to be excused from the financial obligations of membership:

- Suggest that he borrow the money from someone else-- his parents, friends, the credit card company, etc. and owe them instead of the chapter.

- At the next meeting, put $10 in a baseball cap and announce that you are pitching in to pay his bill. Invite those who feels so moved to throw in whatever they feel they can afford.

- Invite his friends to make a motion in chapter to increase each member's bill by the amount needed to cover the bill of their friend who is not paying *or* allocate money from the reserves to cover his bill.

- Point out that there is not just one way to make it through school. Suggest that he move home for a semester and work.

One of my pledge brothers came from a big Irish Catholic family. He was putting himself through school by working in the co-op program and taking part-time jobs during his school terms. When he ran short of money once, he went home to sound his dad out for a loan in a roundabout way. His dad, a WWII vet who had built their house by hand, caught on quickly and would have none of it. "Sounds like you better drop out and work for a quarter," was his suggestion. So that's what he did. What he did *not* do was live in the house and eat meals without paying. This fellow was the President of the Student Government Association, by the way.

Now assuming that the chapter knows what its mission is and how big it needs to be, and it has policies and procedures in place for managing the cash flow, it only needs members. The question is how do we get the guys we are interested in to show up on our doorstep?

▶

RECRUITING

Recruit for contribution and performance

The goal of recruiting is to add new members who will strengthen the organization in ways that support its mission.

It is not hard to pick out chapters that do not recruit for contribution and performance because the one thing they always mention when they are explaining their lackluster recruiting results is *quality*. "We didn't get as many as we hoped for but they are all quality guys. We like them a lot, they like each other and they are fired up about the fraternity."

Really? No kidding? Before this year, did you give bids to guys you didn't like, who didn't like each other and who didn't care much about the fraternity?

Quality in membership terms is not some ethereal concept wrapped up in clichés about brotherhood, the worth of a human life or a person's "impossible-to-quantify contribution to the personal lives of other members." Quality is always in a context and, in the recruiting context, quality is how likely the recruit will be to contribute and perform to the standards of the chapter. If the chapter and member rubrics (samples of which are given in the appendix) are created from the mission statement, then the chapter can easily produce a *recruiting guide* for its members that describes what it seeks in recruits and how that will be determined.

For example, if scholarship is part of the organization's mission then there should be some indication of how scholarship potential is going to be determined in the recruiting guide. If community involvement is part of the mission, then what evidence will the chapter seek that a recruit is predisposed in that direction?

If members know what the organization is about, they can recruit and screen prospects based on how well they think a prospect will help the chapter live up to its mission. This is being *selective*. It is not a license to be snobby. Indeed, if the chapter screened on family or income status, that would reduce the size of the recruiting pool for no reason that serves the members unless they were trying to create a network of rich kids. That is the de facto historical mission of some organizations but they are a minority.

This brings us back to the importance of that mission statement. If your chapter's mission is so broad that it amounts to "surround ourselves with our friends" then you must be prepared for a struggle each year. It is easy for another organization to come along that is just as likable to your prospects and who will get to them first or offer them the same level of "brotherhood", as well as other benefits, for fewer obligations.

Quantity is fundamental

To make a lot of sales, you have to make a lot of calls.

Anyone in sales will tell you that quantity is not the alternative to quality. *Quantity drives quality.* To make a lot of sales, you have to make a lot of calls. A certain number of calls will lead to later steps in the process that ends in a sale. Along the way, prospects drop out because they figure out that they aren't interested in the product. On the other hand, some prospects are dropped from the process because the seller concludes that the product is not suitable or that the prospect *might not be able to meet its obligations to the seller* (as in paying for the product.) In the big world, this is called *The Sales Funnel*. It is illustrated in Figure 5.

Prospects into the Process

⬇ ⬇ ⬇ ⬇ ⬇ ⬇

Selectivity

⬇ ⬇

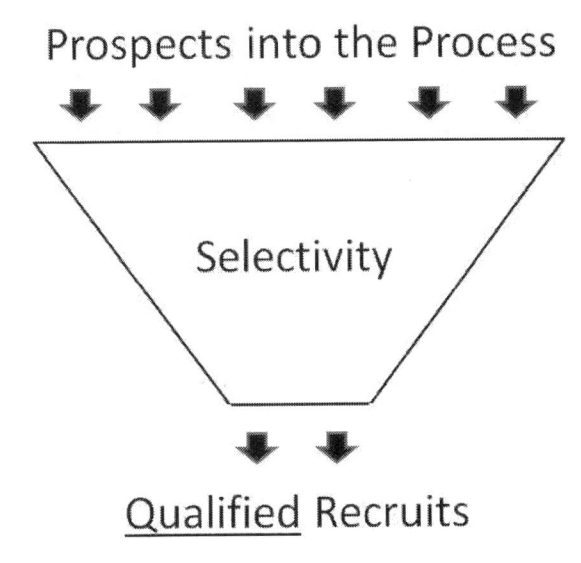

Qualified Recruits

Figure 5. The Sales Funnel

Fill the funnel

It's a lot easier to find what you're looking for if it comes looking for you.

The funnel indicates the first thing that must happen if your chapter is to meet a requirement for a certain number of quality recruits. You must have a lot of prospects.

There are two ways to make this happen. Members can convince prospects to enter the process or prospects can select themselves into the process. Either will do although getting the right people to put themselves into the process is easier on the members and offers greater possibilities for growth.

Think of a college athletic team. The team has a mission—*to win games*. It is easy to measure success. There is no doubt about the criteria. The coaching staff knows what skills and attitudes the team must have to fulfill that mission. Since these skills and attitudes are sought by other teams as well, management cannot wait for good prospects to come knocking. Not even the best teams, those that attract hundreds of hopefuls, do that. All coaches recruit *proactively*. They present their program in the best light to persuade prospects to consider it. The most attractive prospects get personal visits. The coach does not wait for the first day of practice to see who shows up.

Think of your chapter. If the members are sure about the mission, you can put the word out loud and clear so that people who might be interested will be aware of it and select themselves into your recruiting process. The more qualified prospects (as in "prospects who possess desired *qualities*") do this, the more selective your chapter can be. Think of how the Marines recruit, for example. Their advertisements make it clear that physical fitness, taking on challenges and a sense of duty and honor are important to them. Crybabies and lard-butts need not apply. On the other hand, if their ads look like what you want, if they inspire you, then you select yourself into their process.

Contrast this approach with the usual fraternity rush in which chapters simply announce their events, throw open the doors and talk to whomever comes by. Unless the chapter is confident that the people with the qualities it seeks will walk through those doors, it is an unacceptably risky way to find prospects.

Qualify effectively and efficiently

> **Recruit to strengthen the organization.**
> **Develop to build friendships.**

If your chapter accomplishes the first task, it will have its hands full of prospects that it must both sell to and evaluate or *qualify*. If a particular person does not have the qualities the chapter seeks, it would be good to get them out of the process early so that members can concentrate on prospects that do appear qualified. This also points the rejected prospect in directions that are more hopeful for him.

However, it would be a great waste to send a prospect away by mistake. Clearly a lot is at stake during selection. Since the chapter does not have infinite time or manpower, you must have a system that members can use to qualify prospects effectively and efficiently.

Athletic coaches can define *quality* because they know the abilities and knowledge they must see in prospects to develop them as good team members. Recruiting strategy and operations flow directly from the needs of the team. A good coach and his staff know what they are looking for and have learned how to identify the prospects that have the needed skills *and attitudes*-- "coachability", work ethic, ability to balance athletics and academics, and character.

For a fraternity, this is where that recruiting guide comes in again. Since it specifies what the chapter is looking for in members, it can also serve as a guide to gathering information from prospects. And the questions we ask during recruitment will tell those prospects a lot about what the chapter values. Finally, when voting on new members, however it is done, the recruiting guide can frame the discussion, keeping it focused on the potential candidate's likelihood of contributing to the strength of the chapter and away from the personal likes and dislikes of individual members.

However, if you do not get good people into the process, you cannot select them. To increase the chances that you will have a good bunch of recruits, you have to manage your brand.

Manage the brand aggressively

In recruiting, as in love, you must be attractive before you can be selective.

A brand is not a logo or letters or a clever slogan. The chapter's *brand* is the perception of its characteristics and quality in the minds of others. Letters and logos are used to call the brand to mind, which is why they are often confused with the brand itself.

Every action of your members or your chapter may affect your chapter's brand. The actions of members of other chapters may also affect your chapter's brand. Your chapter's brand may affect the opinions others hold about your members or your organization before they have even met you.

Since the brand is a perception, it will be different in each person. That is like saying that, while everyone's experience of the chapter has much in common, each person's experience will still be unique in some ways.

It is not practical to dwell on the perceptions of too many people. So, whose perceptions matter then? The perceptions of prospects matter. And, more, *the perceptions of people who are in a position to influence those prospects matter.* They matter because a chapter with a well-known, strong, attractive brand will have more choices during recruitment than a chapter whose brand is less attractive, is weaker, or is relatively unknown.

Once your chapter is clear about its mission and what it is looking for in new members, it must put the word out there to those prospects and to the people who can influence them. It must say to them all "Hey! If you are looking for this, you have to check us out."

People who have never dealt with your chapter personally should know what it stands for and what it's looking for. They must have a favorable impression of the organization so that they feel comfortable sending sharp guys to it. This starts the process of filling that funnel. A bigger pool of hopefuls means that you can be more selective, which helps you maintain and increase real quality.

Problems with recruiting can be identified by thinking of why that funnel is not filled. Does your chapter:

- Have qualities and characteristics that will attract enough new members or persuade others to refer enough prospects to enable it to fulfill its mission and operate over break-even?

- Have the strength to fulfill its mission well? People like to be part of something that is winning. Success attracts prospects and keeps recruits. Is your chapter's performance good enough to lead people to notice, to talk about it, to spread the word on the chapter's behalf?

- Get the word out in ways (note: *ways* not *a* way) that convey its qualities and characteristics and what it's looking for in prospects to those prospects and to the people who influence them? How does your chapter influence those influencers?

We have addressed the first two points somewhat already. Let us consider the third. To manage its brand well, your chapter must recognize who the prospects and influencers are and devise the best ways to reach them. Where do they hang out? What do they do? What do they look at or read? What matters to them?

Who are those influencers?

To continue, your chapter must be attractive to the next generation of members and to the people who influence them.

What matters to *them*? *To them*? Most organizations are run only in terms of what matters to the current members. That is a strategic mistake if your chapter wants to continue since recruits aren't members yet. You must be concerned with potential members and the people in their lives who can influence their decision to pledge. Examples of influencers include:

- Parents, who have a big influence on finances
- Faculty members and school administrators on campus
- Other students on campus
- Brothers, sisters, and cousins of the prospect
- Friends of the prospect
- The chapter's own alumni who may know the prospect

Other people who might know the prospect or his influencers, whose effects are often great but seldom considered include:

- Students, administrators and faculty members on *other* campuses

- Random people in the community who know the prospect or another influencer
- Random people in other communities who know the prospect

What influences the influencers?

Almost everything about your chapter can affect the brand, depending on whose perceptions are considered. Thinking of these things is like going down a laundry list of chapter quality and risk management criteria. For example:

- Campus and community involvement of members
- How it handles risk management situations
- How it ranks against other organizations in various measures
- How members deal with alcohol
- How members deal with illegal drug use
- How members dress
- How members treat each other
- How members treat non-members
- How members treat other Greeks
- How women are treated
- Its GPA
- Its website content and look
- The activities the chapter participates in
- The behavior of members
- The content of its t-shirts
- The personal bearing or demeanor of members
- The quality of its promotional materials
- The state of its facilities
- Whether it even has facilities
- Whether there have been any "incidents" involving the organization. Etc.

Each of these affects the perception of your chapter in the minds of prospects and influencers. To the extent that it is able, you must think about these things and influence the behavior of your own members in ways that reflect positively on your chapter.

It's happening anyway. You might as well make it work for you. The chapter's handling of issues like these affects its brand even if it doesn't recognize what's going on. This is too important to be left to chance.

It is easy to see when a chapter's brand is lacking. There are few prospects in the process and most of them are the personal acquaintances of current members. To get the numbers it needs, the chapter bids all but the most obviously unsuitable prospects. Excluding a few enables the members (in their own minds) to claim that they are recruiting for quality. In almost every case, however, that quality cannot be defined in terms that related to the chapter's mission. This situation, along with great suggestions for filling the recruiting process with quality prospects, is beautifully described in Mattson and Orendi's *Good Guys*.[14]

Be careful when bidding friends

Membership begins with the fact or possibility of friendship but that is not sufficient for membership.

If someone has joined some wonderful thing, would not it be even better if his friends were in it too? If he has discovered something good, should he not share it with his friends?

---

[14] Mattson, M. & Orendi, J.(2006) *Good Guys*. Naperville, IL: Phired Up Productions.

Traditional recruiting practice is:

1. Get to know the guy,
2. make him a friend, then
3. pledge him!

If he already has done the first two things, isn't the next step to persuade his friend to pledge?

Not necessarily.

Some friends would choose the challenges and obligations of membership in an on-going organization. But many would not. They are ready to have a good time with the members but they lack the desire or the ability to support the organization and pass it on in good shape to others. This does not mean that they are deficient. It is not a reflection on the membership of the chapter. Some friends are just not sold on the idea that joining the fraternity is a better use of their time and money than what they are already doing with those things.

Ability and willingness to support the organization itself are as important as friendship because a fraternity is an ongoing concern. It is not the current generation's "very own fraternity" to use up in pursuit of its immediate personal desires, even the desire to include their friends in a good thing. It is something that was there for them because, in the past, enough members cared enough about the organization to ensure that it would continue. It is something they must pass on to a group of guys they do not even know yet because those guys will not arrive at college for a few more years.

This concept is difficult for members of a colony or young chapter to accept since, at that stage, all the members may be friends. As quickly as possible, however, the new organization must decide what it is about, its mission. From that point forward, it must base its recruiting activities on fulfilling that mission. It must develop members in service to that mission and it must manage its brand to support its new recruiting efforts. Failing to do this is a major cause for the demise of colonies and young chapters.

Don't bid prospects who don't measure up

Sometimes a member is determined to get a bid for a prospect who doesn't measure up. He just likes the guy a lot for some reason. (We called this a "rush crush".) The member may propose to "average things out", to say that weaknesses in some recruits (like his favorite) can be made up by the strengths of other recruits. This introduces a *gaping gap* in membership standards through which people are free to drive a truckload of recruits that they happen to like. This is not fair to the recruits, however.

Each member is expected to live up to minimum standards. To recruit someone into a situation in which he might be found later not to measure up would be unfair to that person and will likely lead to an effort on the part of his friends, and maybe even his parents, to have standards lowered to he can remain a member. It is shortsighted to sacrifice the long-term welfare of the chapter as a whole for the sake of the short-term interests of a particular member or group. Nobody is entitled to that level of consideration.

Remember that friendship is a goal, not necessarily a starting point

Equating membership and friendship can lead us to ignore important considerations during recruiting.

When membership is confused with friendship, naive members bring up their friends for bids, assuming that friendship is all that is necessary. Grades, ability to pay their bills, personal habits that indicate values that agree with those of the organization … none of these matters.

Equating friendship and membership hurts us when the recruiting process focuses *exclusively* on getting comfortable with each other and ensuring a fit based on personality. Nothing about willingness to support what we are as an organization enters into the conversation. Somehow discussing the organization would make the whole process seem artificial and, besides, the obligations of membership might scare away a prospect who is caught up in the idea of being accepted by "his new friends". So it is not discussed or it is a by-the-way thing accompanied by a sheet of paper listing typical dues. The candidate comes in thinking that the fraternity is just a big group of friends, which sets everyone up for unpleasant surprises later if he does not pay his bills or behaves in ways that could be harmful to the chapter. If no one talked to him about the organization itself during recruiting, when was he supposed to find out all that he was signing up for?

This point needs to be made especially to new candidates who are often turned right around during rush into the chapter's most enthusiastic recruiters. At that point in their membership, they are not used to the idea of selective recruiting unless they participated in exclusive sports leagues, for example. Instead they usually are driven to share their new-found wonderful thing with the friends they came from high school with or the guys they have fallen in with in the dorms.

Equating membership and friendship can lead us to be too selective during recruiting.

I remember a member telling his chapter, with good intentions, that he would not give a bid to anyone he would not have as a roommate. Imagine applying that standard for every member in a large, diverse chapter! Not only is it unrealistic, it is arrogant—limiting a chapter's recruitment, the lifeblood of the organization, to the roommate preferences of a single member as if his preferences were always best for the chapter. (I and my best friend from college agree that we became and remain friends only because we never roomed with each other.)

If a prospect does not demonstrate the fact or possibility of friendship among members, then he should not be invited to join. If his attitudes and behaviors indicate that he will not show the same tolerance and respect he will be shown, then suggest that he find a Greek experience elsewhere. But he does not have to inspire the prospect of friendship with every member of the chapter. As long as he treats other members with respect, supports the organization, and behaves in accord with its values, he will become friends with some members and probably get along well with the rest of the chapter. Unless he is habitually unwilling or unable to consider the effects of his actions on others, he will get along. And who knows what the future holds? Changing circumstances may lead to changing relationships. Friendships once close may fade over time while yesterday's mere acquaintance may be tomorrow's best friend.

So the chapter has candidate members. There is a reason, however, for which few important decisions in the world are made by 18-year-olds. At that age, we still have a lot of growing to do. It's in the chapter's interest to make sure that its candidates grow in ways that benefit them and the organization as well. It's also in the chapter's interest to hold members accountable for those behaviors that affect the welfare of the chapter. In the next section, we'll take up development, contribution and performance.

▶

DEVELOPMENT, CONTRIBUTION AND PERFORMANCE

Develop to strengthen the organization

Successful organizations help members develop in ways that strengthen the organization.

We must have missions appropriate for our long-term survival in the current (and changing) environment. Good business sense, as well as a sense of fairness, points to having a development program (DP) in those areas to help initiates become and remain members that support the mission.

This is also a matter of integrity. Are the words of your mission (and your principles) just words or can you point out how they live in your deeds? In everything that the organization says is part of its mission, it must provide for the development of its members. Your chapter must promote personal and professional development that benefit individuals and strengthens the chapter.

To do otherwise is to rely on what new members bring into the organization or develop on their own. But, if we really care about our chapters, can we leave the development of the skills and abilities needed to run them to chance? Does any successful organization do that? Think of a championship basketball team. What does the coach do with new members of the team? Do practice and development stop once tryouts are done? Does he leave it up to the players to work out or not, as they think necessary?

People can and should change from who they are at eighteen. An organization that does not encourage and direct these changes is setting itself up to be outgrown by its best members or used as a sort of Neverland[15] by those who refuse to grow. The role of a member changes from *following* as a younger member to *leading* and being an example of expected attitudes and behaviors as an older member. You must be up-front about this during recruiting, telling prospects that "You will not be the same person in a few years and shouldn't want to be. The environment will change. The chapter will change. You will change."

In the end, developing members well leads a chapter to be more attractive and selective, and it is just one more way in which the chapter can demonstrate to the world that it walks its talk. This is illustrated in Figure 6.

Members must also accept the need to cut prospects that do not fulfill their early promise. This does not mean being quick and ruthless. Some talents are latent; a good team has an organization that can develop them. In the end, though, if the team wants to be successful in terms of its mission, it must be attractive enough to be selective during recruiting then develop

---

[15] The land of Peter Pan, the "boy who never grew up" before it was the name of a famous ranch in California.

members in service to the mission. This increases the chance of success, which enables the team to remain selective, which increases the chance of success, and so on. It a virtuous cycle within the greater cycle of the fraternity for life.

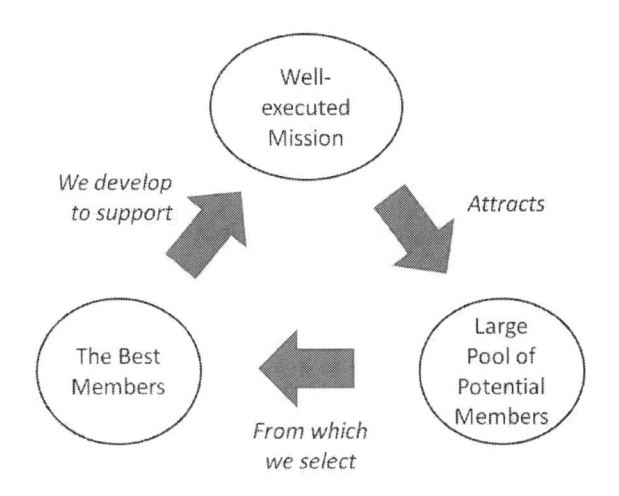

Figure 6. Devlopment and Quality

Promote friendships because the chapter depends on it

Your chapter must regularly carry out activities designed *specifically* to promote the growth of friendships among members.

In all this talk about organizational effectiveness, it is easy to forget the emotional foundation on which fraternities are built. Although we might not all be friends, *fraternities exist to promote the growth of friendships*. Without this, we might as well be professional societies or country clubs. The growth of friendships is too important to be left to chance, i.e. "hanging out with each other." Your chapter must carry out activities specifically designed to:

- lower barriers among members
- help them discover common interests, and
- create trust among members.

Candidates must be involved in such activities with members quickly after pledging. "Pledge class unity" is not important at that time. Friendships among pledge brothers will develop anyway since they are likely to be of similar age and class in school and will probably spend more time together. The goal is to integrate new members into the social life of the *chapter*, to forge *inter-generational* friendships, and to lower barriers that might have developed among older members.

These activities should not be limited to sitting around a campfire drinking beer. Fortunately, there is absolutely no need to reinvent the wheel here. Think about it—for how long have organizations been doing things especially to bring people together? There are many that have stood the test of time and that stand up to today's test of liability: ice breakers, retreats, "paddles"[16], Quaker circles, chapter projects, high and low ropes courses, intramurals, studying together, road trips, etc. National organizations, Greek Affairs Offices and student organizations that stress leadership development are great sources for information on these kinds of activities.

---

[16] Not something that is used to hit anyone with but some symbol of membership that members generally keep on a wall to remind them of the chapter. In my chapter, a paddle could be anything that represented something about the candidate as long as it included the fraternity colors, crest, letters, name of the candidate, etc. We had soccer balls, boogie boards, golf clubs, lanterns, growlers, model cars and airplanes, oriental scrolls, etc. as paddles.

Friendships are not built by throwing big parties, although having fun together moves friendships along. Friendships aren't created suddenly through dramatic events, although such events can break down barriers among members. Friendships are built over years by daily interactions that build familiarity and trust. Members must be comfortable with each other before they'll take that cross-country road trip together or visit each other's families' houses or share a cabin for a spring break cruise. And those activities are the kinds of things that can push friendships along quickly.

Finally, although you may not all necessarily be friends, the more consideration you show each other, the more trust you have in each other, the more you watch out for each other, the better off your chapter will be.

Be clear about expected contribution and performance

People respect what you inspect.

If people know that you are paying attention to how they perform in an area, they'll take care to perform well in that area. Great organizations compare the performance of individual members to organizational standards regularly to recognize people who are doing an outstanding job of supporting the organization and to identify people that need help to bring their contribution and performance into line with what works best for the organization. As with evaluating organizational performance, this is a serious process, deserving some thought.

A Membership Contribution and Performance rubric should relate to the items in your chapter performance rubric and, through that, to the chapter's mission. Keep in mind that this is a contribution and performance rubric, *not* a rubric to measure the quality of friendship or humanity.

As with the Chapter Performance rubric, it is not necessary to measure everything but it should measure the most important things. The areas that the chapter's success depends most on should be translated into specific standards for individual members. Otherwise, officers trying to raise the chapter's performance in a specific area might be left with no way to tell individual members what they need to do differently.

Measurement should be specific. A tolerable measure that can be made 100% of the time without question is better than a perfect measure that can be made 80% of the time. *Keep it simple.* Table 2 shows an example for two dimensions.

Dimension	Satisfactory	Superior
Academics	• On good standing	• On dean's list or higher
Finances	• Meets payment plan	• Pays entire term bill up front

Table 2. Example Membership Contribution and Performance Rubric Items

Performance should have consequences. It is possible to attach a status label to a member based on his performance against the rubric and to attach actions to each status. *Those are totally up to the chapter.* For example (where X represents different numbers the chapter sets):

- **Marginal**: More than X marks less than "satisfactory". Member's conduct or performance detracts significantly from the chapter's ability to fulfill its mission. Membership may be terminated unless significant improvement is seen immediately.

- **Participating**: No more than X marks less than "satisfactory". Member's conduct or performance detracts somewhat from the chapter's ability to fulfill its mission.
- **Satisfactory**: No mark less than "satisfactory". Member does no harm—his conduct and performance support the organization in fulfilling its mission.
- **Superior**: No mark less than "satisfactory". At least X marks of "superior". Member should be recognized by the chapter for going above and beyond in helping the organization fulfill its mission.
- **Exemplary**: No mark less than "satisfactory". At least X marks of "superior". Member is held up as an example to the community and to the recruits as an example of what all members should strive to be.

Do not average performance across dimensions

Satisfactory is the minimum acceptable performance in each area and each member must be satisfactory in every area.

It seems against the idea of looking at "the whole man" but it's bad practice to allow members to make up for weaknesses in one area by being strong in another. If you do this, you will not be able to deal with a failure at the chapter standards level by holding individual members accountable. For example, how could your chapter deal with unacceptable scholarship if each member who was below the individual scholarship standard made up for it by being high on other standards? Instead, set a minimum satisfactory standard that each member must live up to in each area.

This means that you must be careful that satisfactory really represents the *minimum* standard and not what the members would like to see. That level of performance would be *superior*.

As your chapter hones its recruiting and development activities, more members probably will fall into the superior and exemplary categories. Then you might consider raising the bar at both satisfactory and superior levels so that the majority of members fall in the satisfactory range. Note, however, that standards should *never* be reduced. A large number of members not meeting standards points out problems that the chapter should dealt with and not paint over with lower standards.

Hold members accountable for their choices

All organizational behaviors and characteristics flow from the choices of individual members. A chapter that will not hold members accountable for their behaviors will not continue, much less excel, in the long run.

When a person joins a fraternity, he assumes an obligation to act in ways that promote the interests of the fraternity and not to behave in ways that hurt those interests. In return for accepting these conditions, he expects to receive the benefits of membership. Fulfill obligations first. Benefits follow. This is how successful organizations operate.

Fraternities are handicapped in this respect, however, since we have that issue of "brotherhood" thrown in. To many people, brotherhood implies *unconditional acceptance* by the organization and its members. After all, you don't get to pick the guys you share a mother with. That's what many fellows expect when they join a fraternity. They expect a group of friends who will take their side, no matter what. Holding people accountable for anything, be that conduct, grades, or paying dues, is seen as judging or as being "unbrotherly".

Members might even rate the quality of the chapter with how sure they are that, no matter what they do or don't do, there's a place for them in it. To them, "brothers for life" means a lifetime of benefits.

However, they conveniently ignore the other side of the equation—a lifetime obligation to support the organization that made them all brothers. If you asked them whether they thought the chapter had the right to force them to pay dues even if they resigned, they'd look at you as if you were crazy. For them, you see, *unconditional* runs only one way. The chapter cannot make a claim on them but the chapter is obligated to honor their claims on it.

Yet a chapter's characteristics and qualities flow directly from the choices of its individual members. A chapter maintains standards or changes, for better or worse, depending on the attitudes and behaviors of its members. A chapter that wants to maintain standards or improve cannot shy away from holding its individual members accountable for their behavior. A chapter cannot maintain a level of contribution and performance, much less improve, unless it sets aside the idea of unconditional acceptance and enforces standards of individual conduct that line up with the organization's mission and standards.

How accountability often plays out

Friendships notwithstanding, when a person stops fulfilling the obligations of membership, he stops being a member.

At some time, a member may decide to stop contributing to the maintenance of the fraternity. He will have some justification for it. Among the common ones: He cannot afford it. He needs to concentrate on school. His work takes so much time that he has none left for the fraternity. You guys have forgotten what it really means to be a <whatever>. Etc.

If he has decided that he is unwilling or unable to fulfill all the obligations of membership then he should resign. That is not necessarily rejecting the remaining members as friends any more than joining made them friends. He is simply recognizing that he intends to use his time and money differently from now on. It is his choice. It is regrettable but it is his right as long as he is willing to give up the benefits of membership as well.

A problem occurs when somebody will not resign. Maybe he does not like the idea of quitting or of breaking the promises he made when he was initiated. Maybe he fears losing touch with friends. Maybe he is afraid that people will be angry with him. Maybe he wants to keep some benefits of membership without paying for them. Maybe he has persuaded himself, and a few others, of the value of his "intangible contribution to enriching the lives of the members" that is certainly worth more than mere money among brothers.

In the worst case, he will appeal to personal loyalty to avoid being called out. Those closest to him in the chapter may support him. After all, it costs them nothing to plead for him. They do not have to expend the energy to help him live up to the obligations of membership. Their time commitment is over the second you let their friend off the hook. It's a cheap win for them with a high payoff in gratitude from their friend.

Nevertheless, if he will not resign, then the chapter should end his membership.

It is nothing personal. However, he will probably not see it that way and he will make it emotionally as difficult as possible for the chapter, especially the officers. There is no cost to him for doing that. So expect it to be painful. It won't hurt as much if it is dealt with quickly though.

This has happened before. It will happen again. Impartial alumni can help if it is too painful for the officers. Alumni are often aware of past cases that can serve as examples--times when a member was expelled screaming and crying but was soon forgotten and, somehow, the organization managed to continue without the impossible-to-quantify value of his unique contribution.

One of the best lines I have heard an alumnus use to explain the situation to an (ex) member is

> *"I didn't kick you out for not paying your bills. You kicked yourself out when you didn't pay them. I just processed the paperwork."*

That's as matter-of-fact as it can be. But, if things get to this point, you should ask yourself how it came to that.

Freshmen don't arrive at college knowing how fraternities work. They learn from older members. So why did the member expect that he could opt out of one of the basic responsibilities of members? Why did he think that initiation marked the end of his obligation to the fraternity? What signals have members sent to him since he pledged? What examples have members set for him regarding the responsibilities of membership? Did you set him up with unrealistic expectations through your own actions and inactions?

Be honest. The situation did not create itself. Perhaps the chapter needs to be clearer up front about what a member is when the guys they are still candidates and the situation is not muddied by misguided ideas about brotherhood.

Don't bluff

Mandatory behaviors must clearly relate to your chapter's mission so that, if the officers have to come down on a member, it's obviously not personal but about conduct that directly relates to the welfare of the chapter. But be careful what you make mandatory.

> **Do not make something mandatory unless, in the end, you are willing to kick somebody out for not doing it.**

No matter how important or trivial the issue, if something is mandatory eventually someone is going to push the issue-- whether it is paying dues, attendance at chapter meetings, going to study hall, or obeying the no-pets rule in the house. While some people will go along out of a sense of honor or of duty to the organization, others will assume you are bluffing and call you on it. They will refuse to do a thing, and then sit back and wait for your next move. Unless you have the ability to put real pain on such a person, you will not be able to motivate them to comply.

In the big world, if you do not pay even something as small as a parking ticket, when you are found, you may wind up in jail until you pay—and that is just for a parking ticket. Think about it. Behind every small punishment, there is the threat of something much worse. (In business, in the end, they *can* fire you.)

Officers cannot afford to be caught bluffing. If members figure out that you are not willing to sanction someone for failing to live up to a standard or obey some rule, they will start to push in other areas. Eventually, this will undermine any program to maintain or improve performance.

Also, if members know that you have only "nukes or nothing", some may also believe that you will not suspend or expel them for an offence that might be relatively small. Then they really have the leadership in a bind because the rest of the chapter will be watching to see what happens and, without enforcement, the effectiveness of the sanctions as a motivator will be eliminated.

That is why it is good to have toolkit full of intermediate steps—"come to Jesus" talks, fines, and restrictions, for example. But, in the end, the path leads to the door out. Think about this before you make anything mandatory.

Create paths to redemption

You do not owe your members unconditional acceptance. You do not owe them as many chances to live up to your standards as they believe they're entitled to. However, you do owe them clear standards and honest appraisals.

We owe members clear standards and appraisals so that there are no surprises when membership privileges are cut or membership is ended. Membership standards should be in writing. They should be explained during the recruiting and candidate periods. It might be useful to remind members by having them sign an annual agreement acknowledging that they understand the standards.

On the other hand, you need to recognize that people mature at different rates. A few have things figured out before they arrive at college. Others do not really come together until they are well past graduation. Consequently, during our undergraduate years, we do many things that we describe later as "stupid" (when we are in a kind mood.) Fortunately, almost all of us grow. In time, most teenagers who deserve a kick in the head become people anyone would be happy to call friends and neighbors. This suggests the need for ways for members to redeem themselves.

> **You should allow for individual growth in your chapter. Fraternities' declarations of principles usually call this charity, forgiveness or forbearance.**

In the past, advisers just tried to keep undergraduates from harming themselves or others or causing too much property damage until they grew out of it. The challenge these days is to find a way to let people grow in a time when forbearance and forgiveness may be presented in court as abetting and excusing. You must have a process that clearly indicates to members and to outsiders that you enforce limits on behavior but that does not lead you habitually to throw out members who are likely to mature if you are patient with them.

As a leader, you should make no bones about where you are coming from when it comes to protecting the chapter.

> **The organization is more important than the fraternity experience of any particular member or group, even including an entire collegiate chapter. As long as lives are at stake, assets are vulnerable, and money and prison are in the picture, you are justified in disciplining or ending the membership of any initiate whose conduct threatens the life or property of others or of the chapter.**

Failure to enforce an unpleasant consequence for dangerous or illegal behavior will indicate to the members that it's okay and may be used later against the chapter if there is a disciplinary hearing or lawsuit. For the good of the chapter, you must create and enforce consequences that will pass muster in the wider world.

However, where you can, you should create paths to redemption. They should not be garden paths. They should be appropriate for the offense.

Sanctions should be significant.[17] If they were easy, there would be justifiable doubts as to whether the organization took the behavior seriously. There would be doubts about what had changed in a person and his commitment to making good whatever shortcoming he showed. There would be doubts about whether he had truly redeemed himself.

It would be great if the path to redemption could be followed while the person was still a student. However, it might be something that can only be done once he is an alumnus, depending on the behavior. A person may develop late and, as an alumnus, display different attitudes and behaviors. In many cases, some of those old friendships will still be there and may serve as a basis for bringing him back into the chapter, assuming that reconnecting with him would strengthen the organization.

There may be some offenses for which you feel justified in providing no path to redemption, for which separation from the organization is permanent. That's up to your chapter.

Accountability will not be popular. In general, people hope for loyalty instead. For many members, their best friend is "not

---

[17] Be careful about fines. They generally hurt members from poorer families more than those from rich ones. However, this, like all consequences, must be decided for each chapter by the chapter.

the guy who bails you out of jail and helps you make amends but the guy sitting with you in the cell." That's not expecting much of a friend and you don't need to be in a fraternity to have friends like that. *You must hold them accountable anyway.*

Members expect to be shown mercy. Many have been given free second and third chances in failure-proof environments all their lives. They expect the same from the fraternity. They do not accept that there are some screw-ups that are so serious that there must be significant consequences. Saying "I'm sorry" or "Okay, I admit I made a *mistake*" is not significant enough. *You must create those consequences anyway.*

So don't hesitate to point out that you will not give up your ability to govern the organization for the sake of preserving any given person's membership. In the end, you have to be willing to suspend or expel someone who will not comply with a sanction-- not for the original act but for threatening to make the chapter ungovernable and thumbing his nose at a system designed to allow him to redeem himself. Whether such a person could still redeem himself one day would be a matter for the chapter and its board to consider later.

Recognize milestones appropriately

Considering accomplishments, initiation is not as impressive as graduation. You need to make sure that the way you recognize these milestones reflects this.

Place initiation as a beginning, not an end

There is nothing you can and will do legally during candidature and initiation that justifies a lifetime of benefits if those benefits are worth anything.

Initiation should be considered important because it is an acceptance of responsibilities, not a gateway to entitlements. This is counter to almost everything about the way undergraduates usually think of initiation. For them, it is such a big deal because it signals acceptance and is the sole qualification of membership *forever*.

That is a silly proposition—a lifetime of benefits of a few weeks of activity when one is eighteen years old. Not even the Marines or SEALs give that and their programs are much more rigorous than any fraternity pledge program.

Viewing initiation as the only qualification to benefits also encourages hazing because, if membership is worth having and this is the sole way to "earn" it, then all the perceived value of membership has to be piled onto the activities of initiation.

Initiation is the beginning of a long process that should include a development program for members. Celebrate it as such. Then make staying active and advancing through a development program a goal worth pursuing in some tangible way.

Create an alumni scroll

> **Graduation *as a member* is far more significant than initiation. The initiation ritual is a celebration of promises made. The graduation ritual is a celebration of promises fulfilled.**

Signing the chapter scroll or some similar notation of initiation has long been regarded as the symbol of membership attained. No other event in the life of a member carries the emotional weight of initiation. It is staking a claim as part of the history of the organization. However, *graduation as a member* is a far more significant event than initiation.

By member, I mean someone who is paying dues and participating in the activities of the organization. People who signed the scroll but who left or went "inactive" for any reason are not members although they are initiates. They began (initiated) but failed to finish and advance (graduate), you might say. The initiates who graduate are called alumni.

Graduation completely encompasses initiation because it honors the fact of initiation promises fulfilled. To celebrate this, consider creating an alumni scroll or similar document, to be signed or presented at a graduating member's last meeting. Recognition would not depend on level of membership attained (if there are levels), only on having remained a member. The honor *must* be reserved only for those who meet that qualification. There can be no honorary alumni. If you want to honor initiates who are no longer members, then think of another way. But reserve the Big Honor for those initiates who have kept their promises to the chapter no matter what.

Giving someone the honor of signing the alumni scroll, recognizing the greater part of the chapter's history they played, would be a fitting send off for a graduating senior.

In many organizations, hazing is a traditional part of the membership process. Although most hazing is harmless, the legal and technological environment day renders all hazing a risky practice. In the next section, we'll consider why that is and how we must adapt.

▶

HAZING

Nothing interesting stays secret forever

Today's undergraduate students are not wilder than students of previous generations were. It's just easier to document the wildness. With cell phone cameras, any event could be recorded and uploaded without the participants' knowledge. Once something has been uploaded, the owner loses control of its distribution because downloads are as easy as a right-click or tapping the forward button. Even if the material is taken down within minutes, someone might have copied it.

The same technology that supports the spreading of images supports the spreading of video and even just word of mouth. Today's undergraduates are the first generation to live with a reasonable chance of having everything "interesting" they do documented with little or no control over the spread of the record.

Postings don't need to be malicious to do damage. People routinely put up party pictures simply because they are funny without thinking of the possible implications for the people in the photographs. Likewise, members post pictures of secret activities thinking that no one but other members will see them.

These days, believing that you can keep any activity secret indefinitely is, for want of a better word, *stupid*.

Maybe it's hazing.

"The university told ... fraternity members on May 5 their chapter had been suspended for three years following an extensive investigation launched last February ... The investigation began after an anonymous letter accused the WSU fraternity of hazing its members. During the investigation, the university found pictures on Facebook that showed ..."[18]

Maybe it is publicity for a theme party.

"I feel a little sorry for the UC San Diego frat boys who last weekend thought it would be funny to throw a little bash they dubbed the 'Compton Cookout' ... This whole incident might have fallen into the category of frat boys behaving like frat boys if they hadn't made one teensy mistake: posting the event on Facebook. The organizers probably didn't envision the details of their gig ever reaching civil rights groups, the Los Angeles Urban League, Craigslist and even Essence Magazine, which posted an item on its website. The organizer has taken down his profile page, but it's cached. In 5 minutes you can tell not only what his hobbies are (golf) but also where he's from."[19]

Although photographs and videos can be damning, just a few words in the "wrong ear" can be enough to bring unwelcome attention to a chapter. Perhaps a recent initiate makes an offhand remark to his mother about being tired or having to catch up with schoolwork after initiation week. Mom, who is paying for

---

[18] ... closed for hazing. *The Daily Evergreen*. 08/24/2007.
[19] Racist frat boys will be racist frat boys ... on Facebook. *Opinion L.A.* 02/17/2010.

college after all, calls the dean's office to express her concern and the dean starts asking around to see if there is evidence of sleep deprivation. While he's at it, he starts asking whether any brothers showed up with a few six packs. The problems only become worse from there.

But what if someone wants to hurt you or your chapter? Today's happy candidate can be tomorrow's bitter reject. Today's loving girlfriend can be tomorrow's "psycho-ex". What about that obnoxious jerk who showed up uninvited to one of your parties last month and was told to leave? What about that member you kicked out for dealing from the house? Who has a grudge and the goods on your members or your chapter?

Hazing has always been associated with secrecy and the growing difficulty of keeping secrets poses a strategic threat to any organization whose identity depends on hazing.

Before you insist that your chapter is stronger than that, ask yourself how your membership would react if you eliminated every activity from retreats and initiation that you would not allow parents and administrators to witness. Would current members object, "If they don't do what we did, they'll never really be accepted into the brotherhood."? If the answer is yes, then your chapter probably defines membership through hazing.

Unfortunately for such chapters, the inability to keep things secret has occurred at the same time and possibly has helped drive the growing intolerance of administrators and national offices for any kind of activity that smells remotely like hazing. Thanks to a steady stream of deaths like the one in 2011 at FAMU, and the criminal charges and lawsuits that follow each, hazing is in the spotlight. Given the environment, a chapter that makes hazing an integral part of its identity is committing a huge strategic error.

To rely on secrecy is a potentially fatal strategic weakness for an organization.

If your chapter or its members habitually engage in activities that, if made public, would lead to the closure of the chapter or to members being disciplined by the school or charged with crimes, then your chapter is skating on thin ice. *All such activities must stop.*

Scenario

You are the president of your chapter. You awake one morning to discover that you have an appointment with the assistant dean of students for Greek affairs. It seems that one of your candidates, normally a good student, bombed a test. When the professor asked him whether anything was the matter and whether he needed any help, the student responded that no, he was fine, but he had just been through initiation last week. The professor has nothing against the Greek system but, unhappy that one of his best students has just bombed a test, he mentions the incident to the Greek dean. The dean goes over a list of chapters who were initiating last week and finds yours. All of your new initiates and all former candidates who dropped out of your program, including those you told to leave because you discovered that they were jerks, receive notices to schedule individual appointments with the dean.

- *Scenario A: Your candidate program is full of local rituals that involve blindfolds, alcohol, pranks on other chapters, curious activities "out in the county", and sleep deprivation.*

- *Scenario B: All activities of your candidate program have been vetted by your school and by headquarters. The outline is published on-line and the chapter does not deviate from it. You invite parents, administrators and alumni to participate in public aspects of your program.*

In which scenario do you feel more comfortable meeting the dean?

The fight that is never finished

If hazing is such a problem, why does it persist? Set aside loose statements that link hazing with insecurity or low self-esteem. That's talk by counselors for counselors and an amateurish attempt at shaming. As for "Is that how you would treat a brother?", well, in fact, for decades that is exactly how brothers treated each other and, in the overwhelming majority of situations, with no obvious harm done.

Hazing is often presented as a rite of passage. Such activities have been around for millennia. If they were, per se, destructive in organizations, then many of our institutions would have collapsed long ago. An intense common experience associated solely with the attainment of membership can be a bonding experience as well as engender loyalty to an organization. These are good things to have, as anyone who has watched "Band of Brothers" will tell you. People have compared hazing to the rigors of boot camp or plebe year, in which one proves he is qualified to serve in the military. In "Band of Brothers", the harsh conditions at Camp Toccoa, followed by their common struggles as they fought their way across Western Europe definitely created a wonderful bond.

So what's the problem with trying to do the same thing in a fraternity by creating some obstacles to overcome as a condition of membership? Wouldn't it be good to make them earn membership by proving they are qualified for it?

The problems with hazing in fraternities

The first problem with fraternity hazing, compared to the military boot camp example, is what is meant by "qualified" and "earn".

Allowing yourself to be hazed doesn't prove anything but that you want membership.

Soldiers work with weapons; they make decisions with serious consequences every day. As part of the military's mission, they must be willing to take lives and, perhaps, to sacrifice their own. They must learn to follow orders. Their lives may depend on reacting without thinking. The rigors of boot camp are designed to help people develop in service to the military's mission and to certify them as ready to play their part in fulfilling it.

Fraternities also have missions but *there is no relationship between traditional hazing practice and the ability to fulfill the mission.* Instead, the purpose of going through fraternity hazing is nothing more than *to demonstrate how much you want to be a member.* That is all there is to prove. Submitting to hazing is a means of gaining acceptance, nothing more.

However, having "endured the test" does not certify one as qualified to do anything except, perhaps, turn around and help haze the next group. An initiate's desire for membership, as evidenced by his endurance of hazing, does not indicate that he will be a competent member. He may simply be that tough or that desperate for acceptance.

Most undergraduates don't have enough life experience to conduct a rite of passage.

The second problem with fraternity hazing has to do with who does it. If you consider old societal rites of passage or the military's boot camp, these institutions are run, not by those who are close in age and development to the inductee, but by older members of the society. With maturity comes perspective. What are we really trying to accomplish here? What are the risks associated with this practice and do the benefits justify them? How would these activities play in the bigger world?

In the military, a drill instructor must take an intense course in order to be qualified to train those that are coming into the military. Instructors are extremely aware of injuries that have happened to their soldiers and, although they push them to their limits, they are also aware that harming them does not strengthen the military branch they are in; it actually weakens it.

In a fraternity, however, a person is put through the rites by people barely more mature than he is, whose perspective is barely broader than his is, if at all, and whose only training is having been through it themselves.

Hazing encourages an entitlement mentality.

The third problem is the mentality that hazing engenders in initiates. Hazing allows people to indulge in the *fantasy* of having earned membership, after which they feel entitled to the benefits no matter what. They believe they have already paid for them by enduring the hazing. This is the "entitlement mentality".

If we were able and willing to run candidate programs like real boot camps or plebe years, a sense of having accomplished something worthwhile in exchange for which one is now entitled to something might be reasonable. But we do not. Anything we can do in candidacy and initiation is a feeble imitation, *a child's game*, compared to military indoctrination or a real purposeful experience such as Airborne School or the Crucible Experience of the Marine Corps.

Nevertheless, we have probably all heard some version of, "The last time I looked, my name was on that scroll so get off my back." That is a destructive attitude, and removing any notion of having "earned" membership through being hazed is a step in the right direction to completely invalidating it.

Hazing tends to get worse over time.

The fourth problem is that hazing tends to get worse over time. *No chapter is founded as a hazing organization.* It creeps in as undergraduates imitate stereotypes or other organizations. It only takes a little "harmless" hazing activity to get things started. Then the next group of candidates, well, they cannot do less to earn this membership, can they? And now the chapter is on the slippery slope of escalating hazing practice. The sad thing is that the changes will probably be small from year to year but, over the years, the differences add up to something that would be alien to the chapter's founders. When the situation finally blows up, the undergraduates are genuinely confused because, after all, what they were busted for was not much worse than what was done to them. As far as they know, "it has always been done this way and there were never any problems."

Hazing sets your chapter up to be blackmailed.

Finally, given today's laws, hazing practice gives every associate and every member the evidence to blackmail or bring down the organization. A phone call or photograph from a disgruntled associate, parent, or ex-girlfriend to certain people can have the whole organization hauled into a judicial process and suspended or dissolved.

If you came down on someone for failing to fulfill the obligations of membership when that person felt entitled to those benefits because he was hazed, should you be shocked if he "rats you out" in anger? If you cared about an organization, would you put such power into the hands of any one person, especially a person who had a bone to pick with the organization?

How can a leader manage an organization full of members who feel entitled? How can the leadership hold members accountable if the organization can be blackmailed or destroyed by any of them?

Furthermore, no faculty or alumni adviser would want to be associated with a chapter that is known for hazing, much less make a substantial investment of time or money to it. The risks are too high—and for what? What benefits of hazing could justify placing the charter, the building, the reserve fund, and the futures of members in jeopardy?

If an activity is illegal per se, dangerous to a reasonable person, or immoral in the eyes of the initiate, it should not be done. Would you videotape it and show it to a potential employer, to your parents, to your classmates?

If you keep it secret because of what people might say or do to you or to the organization (or what the law might do) then it should not be happening. No one test is perfect, depending on how "free" your spirit is. Some people would not be bothered by anything. So use several tests. And you can always test the activity against your mission. Does it prepare a member to serve the mission? If not, you should probably think of something else to do.

A candidate or pledge *cannot* consent to hazing and, yes, a chapter can be charged with hazing a brother.

There is no document that a candidate or member can sign that will keep the chapter from being charged with hazing if the activity fits the definition.

The standards that apply to hazing candidates or pledges also apply to brothers. So you cannot make a given activity allowable simply by moving it to an "optional" status that takes place a few weeks or months after initiation. It's the nature of the activity, not just the threat of withholding membership, that makes it hazing.

Emphasize privacy instead of secrecy

Violation of secrecy makes the chapter look bad. Violation of privacy makes the teller look bad.

Abandoning secrecy does not mean that everything is out in the open. The alternative to secrecy is privacy. Secrets are kept out of fear of consequences to the organization but privacy is kept out of respect for each other. The respect is *personal*, and privacy goes hand-in-hand with trust among members—a quality you should build through your activities.

For example, many organizations have a retreat or initiation activity that includes answering a series of questions within the confidence of the group. The session usually starts with light-hearted inquiries such as "your most funny embarrassing moment" but can end many hours later with questions that get to the heart of life-changing events members have experienced. Done well, it can be an effective and valued activity for breaking down barriers among members.

It should be no secret that a chapter has such an activity, but individual responses to questions should remain *private*. Some family matters, reactions to dramatic events in one's life, things we have done and are not proud of but learned from, unrealized hopes and dreams—all of these are candidates for privacy.

Consider the position of a person who violates an assumption of secrecy compared to someone who violates an assumption of privacy. When a chapter secret is exposed, it could be awkward for some people and certainly they will be angry. However, nothing personal has been revealed except what might be inferred about the members from nature of the activities they participated in. From the outside, the teller has not crossed that line of personal confidence. "Well, y'all shouldn't have been doing that" will be the response from the big world to the members' outrage about the leak.

On the other hand, has someone ever told you something about another person that you really felt you should not be hearing? What do you believe about the teller as a result? Would you trust that person with something important to you or about you? Revealing things said under an assumption of privacy is a personal betrayal and people of good character will see it as such.

There are limits to privacy, however. Some years ago, an initiate had mentioned to some other members during a private event that he had been under treatment to help him deal with thoughts of suicide. A few years later, that person was facing disciplinary action from the chapter's board. Although the members were clearly uncomfortable doing it, a few of them mentioned that they feared for his safety and wellbeing. They told the board about his earlier revelations and the board changed completely its approach to dealing with the situation.

It wasn't pleasant for anyone but it was the right thing to do. *Nothing* comes before the safety and wellbeing of people and, sometimes, our choices are between two painful alternatives. That's just life.

Be aware then. No one can render an incident or topic off-limits for discussion outside the organization simply by talking about it during a private event. Especially law-breaking or incidents or conditions that call into question the safety or wellbeing of anyone may certainly be discussed with advisers, parents, school administrators and law enforcement officers if it is appropriate. There can be no "wall of secrecy" or "sacred bond" protecting any and all acts of a member simply because they are members. There can be no such protection for the activities of the chapter either.

If the chapter is not hazing, it has greatly lowered the chances that it will have a bad encounter with the dean or headquarters. Still, the chapter's activities will always bump into the interests of other players in the environment. What can we do to make it more likely those are pleasant encounters? Also, no organization of a few dozen men whose membership turns over completely every few years has in it everything it needs to survive every challenge it will face in the long run or to take advantage of every opportunity that appears. How can a chapter secure those other resources?

▶

A COMMUNITY OF STAKEHOLDERS

In the late 1990s, I visited a chapter at a small school about an hour and a half from my house. The group had had membership and financial issues for a long time. I had over fifteen years of chapter advising experience. There was no local alumni support. The lead volunteer in the state asked me to see whether there was something we could do to help them since otherwise headquarters would take back the charter soon for failure to pay dues and insurance.

I hit the road after a day's work at my regular job. It was getting dark as I pulled up to a trashy little cinder block house off campus. Six or seven undergraduates waited in the living room—about thirty percent of the membership.

They knew why I had come and they were wary. They hardly talked until I pointed out that I was not from "nationals" but a local volunteer. The president seemed bright and spoke well but none of the other officers had brought their work as I had asked. They were not prepared to answer questions about the chapter's operations.

Nevertheless, I gradually teased enough out of them to see a big strategic flaw in their recruiting strategy. I pointed out some different possible approaches and made suggestions in that area and others--nothing big but some things that would at least get them moving forward again. However, for every action I proposed, however small, they had a reason for which it could not be done or would not work.

After a few rounds of the suggestion-objection game, it was obvious to me that they wanted things to *be* different but they had no interest in *doing* anything differently. Finally one fellow made a suggestion in a by-the-way manner as he ducked behind a couch to pick something up off the floor.

"Well we *might could* do something if we could get a little alumni support," he said.

I wondered what he thought I was. Then I realized what he meant. They wanted money.

Why in the world would an adult give the time of day to these people, I wondered, *and why am I still here?*

On the other hand, from their point of view, what was I but a stranger who had suddenly showed up to look at what they were doing. I was probably a threat to what little they had going on even if I was a volunteer of the organization that they supposedly represented on their campus. Why were they not used to dealing with adult volunteers? *Where were their own alumni?* Why were they not able and willing to help them?

Does this sound like some chapters you know?

Alumni and the school's Greek administration are two stakeholder groups that can be great help to a chapter if they choose but who also can shut it down if they believe it's in their best interests. It's worth your time to think about how you are dealing with them.

Think of alumni and volunteers as customers

Don't expect alumni donations of time and money unless your chapter becomes a more attractive use of those things than alternatives.

A business should know who its customers are. It's obvious that current and potential members are, in some ways, customers since you have to spend time thinking about what they want and how to make your product attractive to them. However, current students are not your only customers.

All fraternities say they are "for life" and yet, for most of our existence, we have put little thought into how to make our product attractive to our alumni. Yet there are so many more of them than there are undergrads. They are more knowledgeable, have more contacts and they are wealthier. We ask them for money and time that they could donate to other causes, which makes them our customers as well.

No chapter thrives for long without frequent, intimate adult involvement. National organizations know this so they are always trying to convince alumni to get involved. So why does every chapter not have a strong board of a dozen alumni to guide it? Why aren't alumni falling over themselves to help? After all, most alumni have happy memories of undergrad life and they are familiar with the nature of the work through their own collegiate experiences.

Familiar with the nature of the work—maybe that is the problem. Alumni know what the typical chapter is about and, despite their fond memories and feelings, they have concluded that they have better things to do with their time than to support collegiate social fraternities. Otherwise, national offices would be turning them away from volunteer positions. If more alumni thought the fraternity was a relatively attractive use of their money, the Greek system would receive more donations.

If you want to change this for your chapter, you must set aside the old practice of running your chapter as if it were a purely collegiate organization—by undergrads, for undergrads. Instead, run the chapter as an organization that brings students and alumni together in a mutually beneficial relationship. Ironically, this amounts to thinking of what you must do to become what every national fraternity says it is—something for life.

As a system, we must change if we are to fulfill our potential as organizations. If we are for life, we must found chapters that are built to provide a lifelong experience from the moment the interest group is formed. If we are for life, each candidate must see his collegiate experience as a stepping-stone to alumni involvement from the day he pledges. If we are for life, we must create a desirable evolution after graduation to alumni association membership and to continuing support of and benefits from involvement with the Chapter.

Fortunately, putting into action the practices and policies that have been described in this book would give you something that alumni could support with time and money: having a clear attractive mission, demonstrating that you walk your talk, paying attention to the brand, running the chapter like a well-run business, and having a program that develops members in ways that anyone can see is beneficial. As important, these actions create a framework for managing alumni involvement by suggesting opportunities for the training, mentoring and facilitating that alumni can provide.

Become a fraternity for life

Old model

In the old model of fraternity, a chapter starts as a group of students who want to organize. At some point, they approach a national organization. If the group seems like a decent bunch of fellows, they will be allowed to open a franchise of the national, which gives them operational support and guides them through the chartering process. Sometime during this process, someone looks around to "find some alumni to help these guys out" and they become the thin red line that stands between the organization and the occasional brush with oblivion.

As long as the group operates, collegiate members form friendships with each other, sometimes between different generations in the chapter. These overlapping groups emerge with each graduating class and spin off into the big world. Individuals keep up with their close friends in many cases. Gatherings such as tailgates and golf tournaments occur occasionally, mostly organized by these groups. There is no overall organization of the alumni. A new graduate steps into a limited network of personal friendships. At homecoming, he might go by the House and have a look around but he will hang out with the guys he knew when he was a collegiate member. For him, they are the fraternity. This situation is illustrated in Figure 7

What is the role of the volunteers in this model? It has been described as "riding herd" but that is being generous. Cowboys riding herd lead the group (of cows) to their ultimate destination. Along the way, they anticipate difficulties and guide the herd around them. They make the big picture decisions. What goes on in the herd is up to the cows as long as they are not creating issues for the cowboys. If a few cows step out of line, they are turned back into the herd. Occasionally it is necessary to cut one out--perhaps it is incapable of finishing the journey--but that is just part of the job.

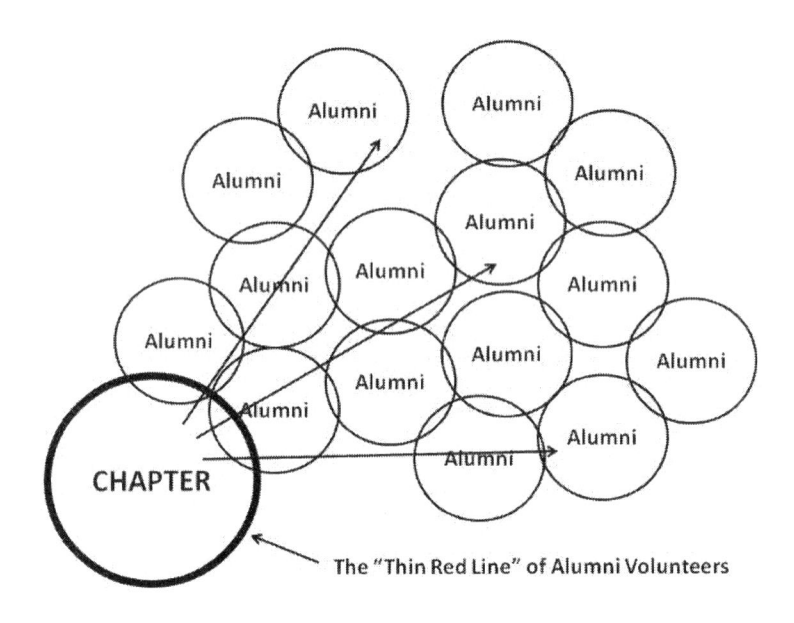

Figure 7. The Old Model of Fraternity

In the old model of fraternity, volunteers have a difficult time exercising even that level of oversight. The herd goes where it wants, reacting only to immediate concerns and problems instead of anticipating them. Occasionally something looks particularly interesting or frightening and there is a stampede. The cowboys do nothing in particular until something bad happens. Then they ride in and rescue the (temporarily) grateful and cooperative cows. The herd mills around a bit and then starts in the most interesting direction again. The cowboys retreat until the next crisis.

That is not a good use of the time of a skilled cowboy. Basically, it is a job with no goal. It feels good the first time or two he "rescues" the herd but that feeling wears off quickly especially when he figures out that he is almost powerless to prevent crises from happening repeatedly. Given the many dangers that face herds today, both environmental and from "cows with issues" inside the group, this model presents an even less attractive opportunity to qualified cowboys.

How many will sign up to ride herd on a collegiate social fraternity? In the Greek world, evidence suggests that very few do relative to the number of alumni we have produced.

Both the adviser experience and the alumni experience must change.

A fraternity for life

If you want your chapter to succeed in the long run, design and build it to be attractive, not only to current and future students, but to the *best kind of alumni and other adults* as well. If you want people to be involved for a lifetime, create an experience that is gratifying at each stage of a person's life. To make this happen, create a chapter around values and programs that adults will support.

It is not a mystery what those values and programs are. Here are some based on a survey of alumni I know who, by the way, were no group of angels when they were undergraduates:

- ***Achievement in scholarship.*** This is by far the most important thing to alumni in general. Does the chapter actively support the academic success of its members? Serious tuition dollars are on the line.
- ***Be involved in the school and community.*** The organization should matter. Members should be playing important roles in good things that are happening on campus

and in the community. This is one of the reasons for which philanthropy and community service are so important.
- ***Keep social behavior under control.*** "Social out of control" is a red flag to alumni, except possibly for a few who have nothing better to do than go back down to the house and play beer pong with undergraduates. Regardless of their own conduct as students, alumni are not eager to support organizations whose members are habitually drunk and obnoxious in public and whose brand includes wild parties and a strong alcohol component. This does not mean "no alcohol" but "keep it between the lines".
- ***Stay out of trouble with the administration.*** A record of problems is an indicator of other things going wrong, especially regarding academics and behavior.
- ***Take good care of the facilities.*** If the chapter has a house, keeping it clean and in repair shows pride in the organization and says something about the character of its members. Especially if the alumni helped acquire or improve the facilities, how they are used and maintained is important. "I won't give a dime to help out a kid who won't put a beer can in a trash can," is how I heard one alumnus put it.
- ***Financial stability.*** With the exception of major capital campaigns for facilities and scholarships, chapters should "pay as you go". Financial troubles are a red flag, possibly in several areas including membership levels and organizational competence.
- ***No hazing.*** Regardless of what they went through themselves as undergraduates, most alumni understand that public opinion has changed and that legal liabilities exist. Who wants to have his name associated with acts that are now banned by all national organizations and illegal in most states? Who wants to donate time and money to an organization that engages in activities that could endanger those investments?

- ***The deportment of individual members.*** An alumnus should be able to sit and talk with any senior in the chapter and conclude that this is the kind of person he would want his children or grandchildren to be around or that he would want to hire or have as a colleague. All members should be polite but the character of the seniors--those who have been under the organization's influence for several years--should shine. "I want to see in the seniors the kind of young man I'd want my kid to become," said one alumnus.
- ***Diversity of backgrounds.*** Regardless of the composition of the chapter when they were students, most alumni recognize the value to the organization and to its members of drawing from a diverse pool of potential members. The composition of the world is changing, as is that of our country and our schools. Our organizations should reflect this change if we want to take full advantage of the potential of today's youth and prepare our members to be effective in the changing world.

A chapter of these qualities differs from the stereotypes of fraternities and how we are portrayed in the movies and on TV. For your chapter, maybe this list represents a total rejection of your current attitudes and behaviors. Yet, if you are to become "for life" and reap the benefits of greater alumni involvement, your chapter must honor the things that your alumni value. Only then can you expect substantial support from them. The same goes for adults who are not your alumni.

A superior model of fraternity is one in which the collegiate years are seen as the gateway to a lifetime of involvement that benefits *all* members. Instead of a fraternity experience that ends at graduation and is replaced by a circle of close friends, the idea of *membership* remains. Send your graduates into a network of professional and personal help in which there are plenty of opportunities to both give and receive help and information.

Initiation, once the most significant event in the fraternal experience, would be seen as the important *first step* in the journey of a lifetime. Graduation, currently a farewell ceremony in which the emphasis is on what one leaves behind, would become instead a transition to another stage of involvement, a walk through a gateway and onto a longer, wider path. Figure 8 illustrates this kind of organization.

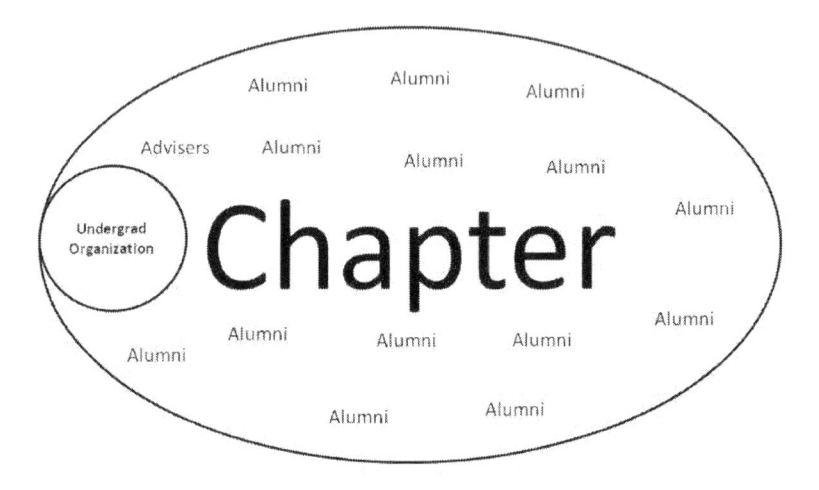

Figure 8. A Fraternity for Life

Empower an alumni board to help you

An alumni board should perform the same function for the chapter that a corporate board performs for a well-run corporation.

For most of our history in most chapters, advisory boards practiced only loose oversight of chapter operations. Facilities issues were a matter of benign neglect. Every now and then, the chapter ran up debts it could not pay and required an intervention, after which it would go back to whatever it was doing before.

Undergraduates resisted more oversight and it has long been difficult to find alumni willing to become involved, so small were the gratifications of showing up once or twice each term to intrude where they were generally not welcome unless there was an emergency. Most undergraduates saw no advantage, except possibly financial, in cooperating with their alumni. History shows us that this is not a good use of sharp alumni.

A board should supervise to the extent necessary to make sure that the organization performs its mission. The board should intervene when the organization appears to be straying, that is, when the train begins to wobble--not after it is clear that it has jumped the tracks.

Some disconnected alumni sniff at the idea of oversight. They ask, "Aren't you denying them the opportunity to learn from mistakes the way we did?" This question displays a lack of experience with the current environment.

If it were only a matter of the personal liability of the students, then alumni could sit back, let people screw up, and watch as they and their parents dealt with the legal and financial fallout. But it is not these days. Organizations take on legal obligations on behalf of their members—musical group performances, facilities contracts, and housing loans for example. Lawsuits follow the money and, if the organization has assets, a savings account or house for example, they may be seized to honor those obligations. Lawsuits having to do with hazing, assault, injury, harassment, etc. follow the money as well.

It makes no sense to expect adults to put their names to documents to help a chapter buy a house and then leave the welfare of the group totally up to the unsupervised choices of a group of typical twenty-year-olds. Some formal oversight is necessary—that performed by a well-run corporate board.[20]

Undergraduates will always find mistakes to make. A board should act to keep those mistakes from being of the kind that endangers the entire operation. Here are the activities of a competent board:

1. **Provide consistency over the long term in the areas of strategic planning.** Alumni volunteers ensure that the collegiate organization lives up to the expectations of its alumni and continues to provide new graduates who can and will add to the strength of the social network. Collegiate members are not in a position to do this. Only alumni are positioned to maintain focus over the years and bring a historical perspective to decision-making. This means that it is the responsibility of the alumni board to look at the environment, think, and have a well-conceived strategy for the organization. But even the most astute alumni don't necessarily understand everything that his happening on the ground. So a well-run board will include the undergraduates on discussions of these topics so that the alumni can

---

[20] Not the kinds of corporate boards that helped bring about the financial crisis of 2008 by not exercising competent oversight.

understand the day-to-day reality of life on campus and the collegiate members start to see the big picture.

2. **Preserve and transmit improvements.** This gives the chapter a chance to be improving continuously instead of reinventing the wheel. How many times have you seen one slack officer destroy years of accumulated good knowledge and practice, necessitating an intervention, clean-up, and retraining from scratch?

3. **Prevent one generation from passing on problems to the next.** This is huge and can be used to cover a multitude of things chapters are used to sweeping under the carpet—members' behavioral issues, big chapter debts, unfunded maintenance needs, etc. A board insists that each generation solve the problems it creates and deals with the issues it faces. This is superior training for life. It is also a purpose whose benefits the current generation can understand, especially if things are going well. A well-run board includes the undergraduates on discussions on these topics so that the collegiate members start to understand the importance of planning and precedents.

4. **Be a source of advice and expertise,** a pool of speakers, providers of contacts with other alumni, and a source of career and personal mentors and *advisers*. Adult volunteers should model the attitudes and behaviors of members toward other members. They should help identify and guide the development of potential leaders.[21] They should serve as "grownups who will tell you what your parents would only

---

[21] Guiding development and participating in the program will be easier if there is an established development program that makes sense to adults—something they can see real value in. This points out the possible use of a Development Program (DP) as a framework for getting alumni involved.

you'll listen because they're not your parents." Adults can help collegiate members develop a sense of perspective, especially about problems and what's important in life. (I remember the look in the eyes of my chapter's undergraduates the first time the chapter was put on social probation for scholarship. Later, one of them told me that they were in a panic, thinking it was the end of the chapter, until they looked over at the alumni who sat calmly, saying, "We've dealt with a lot worse. It's not the end of the world. We'll come through it fine.")

Basically, alumni involvement comes down to services, standards and development—delivering services to the chapter, enforcing standards and helping members develop. Rather than letting the undergraduates learn by making mistakes that endanger the organization and the experience of the next generation, a board makes the chapter a place in which students learn by modeling behaviors that work. They teach the undergraduates the right way to steer the ship so that, when storms blow in, the chapter can more quickly find a way out of them. And, yes, undergraduates will still make mistakes. But they will be less likely to make ones that will sink the ship.

Start a chapter with an alumni association

Create organizations from the beginning to do things that attract alumni involvement or, at least, do the kinds of things that alumni would want to be associated with. Include alumni association planning from day one in a colony and introduce it to existing chapters, even if it is not an "official" association. This should include, at least, a member database suitable for tracking alumni data as well as collegiate data, a community communications instrument of some kind, whether print or on-line, and social media groups to support keeping in touch and finding employment or services.

Fortunately, information technology makes it easy and inexpensive to keep up with large groups of people. We are a long way from abandoning printed newsletters but even those are less expensive to produce than in the past.

Finally, in honor of becoming an organization that is truly for life, start measuring chapter success not by the number of new pledges or initiates each term, but by the percentage of initiates who graduate as members (i.e. paying bills) and then contribute financially or with hours to any level or activity of the fraternity. That would demonstrate the virtuous cycle is operating. That would show that the fraternity really is for life.

Cultivate relationships with external stakeholders

To get along with any stakeholder group, find out what their problems are and offer them solutions instead of more problems.

Other than alumni and undergraduate members, there are important stakeholders that have no particular emotional attachment to the chapter, such as campus administrators, the local police, and the neighbors. The secret to getting along with them can be discovered by understanding what forces affect their own wellbeing and what problems they are facing, and then finding ways to help them deal with those forces and problems. In other words, put yourself in their shoes and look at your organization as they see it. *It's just that simple.*

Scenario

You are the president of your chapter. You awake one morning to discover that you have an appointment with the assistant dean of students for Greek affairs. It seems that while you slept a couple of sophomores decided to steal a few items from one of the neighboring chapter houses. By the way, they also left the water running through a hosepipe leading to the neighbor's basement. The new carpet in their party room is soaked. It's already started to stink.

- *Scenario A: When you took office, you held a meeting with the dean to introduce yourself and to get her opinion of your organization and how it stacks up against the others on campus. Since then, you have held bi-weekly meetings with her even if only to chat about things on campus in general. Once or twice, you have brought along your educator or treasurer or social chair so they can get to know her since they will likely stand for your office in the next election. Your chapter regularly participates in substance abuse, scholarship, and leadership development activities sponsored by her office. Your chapter GPA exceeds the male average.*

- *Scenario B: You have never met the Greek dean. Your chapter participates in nothing her office provides. Your chapter GPA is below the male average.*

In which scenario do you expect to get the benefit of the doubt from the dean? If your chapter is found responsible, in which scenario do you expect to get the lighter sanction?

Now replace the dean with the chief of police, the chair of your board of advisers, and the old man who lives down the road in the neighborhood your chapter house is in. If you need their help, under which scenario are they more likely to give it?

If the only time an administrator hears about a chapter is when it has screwed something up, why should they be friendly and helpful to that organization? Would it not be better to remain in regular communication with the administrator through good times and bad?

Find out how Greek administrators are reviewed and rated by their bosses. Then figure out how to help them get good reviews. Be a solution to their problem instead of something that makes them look bad to their bosses and to the community. Odds are that your Greek administrator is being evaluated by criteria including such items as how the fraternities are doing academically, the number and nature of disciplinary or other incidents, how the Greek houses look on Sunday mornings, how much philanthropy and community service the fraternities do, how involved the Greeks are with student government and other campus organizations, etc. Does this list look familiar?

Find out whether the administrator needs a fraternity to step up to work with freshman move-in or with a non-profit in the community. Would they look good if a fraternity adopted a road near campus? Would their bosses smile if they had huge attendance at a seminar on alcohol abuse?

If a potentially serious incident occurs at your house or involves one of your members, make sure the dean hears about it from you first.

Keep those channels of communication open. Especially if a potentially serious incident occurs at your house or involving one of your members, let the dean hear about it from you first. Don't keep your head down hoping it will pass unnoticed because, if it doesn't, the first report to the dean will likely come from the other side of the incident or from the police. She'll have their version of it first and that will bias how she hears yours. Also, it makes you look like you are trying to hide something. Just make the call or send the e-mail and get it over with.

The same goes for faculty, for the police and for neighborhood associations.

Police officers are used to dealing with liars, the "impaired" and smart-alecks. Imagine how most officers would react if you treat them with respect, especially if your organization has a long history of dealing with the police in a forthright manner.

Scenario

It's 2:00 am and the party inside has been going on for hours. A police officer shows up at the door, saying there's been a noise complaint. He asks to come in. The president calls the chapter adviser: Remember. It is two o'clock in the morning.

- *President (upset): Hey Ryan, I'm sorry to bother you but there's a cop at the door and he wants to come in!*
- *Adviser (calm but sleepy): Yeah, so what's the problem?*
- *President: Well we've been partying all night. The house is full of kids.*
- *Adviser: Okay, so what's the problem?*
- *President: He wants to come in! What do I tell him?*
- *Adviser: You tell him, "Come in, officer."*
- *President: But what if he walks around? The house is full of kids. You know, stuff's going on. Kids are drinking.*
- *Adviser: You think the cop doesn't know that?*
- *President: But what happens if he sees something?*
- *Adviser: Then he might write you up or he might not. Whatever it is, we'll just have to deal with it in the morning.*
- *President: Couldn't I just tell him no?*
- *Adviser: Sure, and then he'll see something over your shoulder that gives him probable cause and he'll come back in a few minutes with two or three of his buddies. They'll be pissed and they* will *find something. Is that what you want?*

The cop came in, walked around, wrote a few kids up for underage drinking and told the boys to lower the volume a bit.

Everyone knows that undergraduates drink but a typical police officer has many other things he could be doing than busting students for underage drinking as long as there are no other problems. It's when students get drunk and act like jerks that the police must get involved. If your members drink, can you make sure they exercise a little sense when they do? Can you insist that they not behave in ways that compel officers to act? Wouldn't that be good stuff for them to know anyway?

Neighborhood associations will be against anything that threatens property values or that makes people feel unsafe, especially where children are concerned. Generally, chapter houses are not good neighbors because they work against both of those things. Property owners are willing to sacrifice every ounce of joy you may find in your lifelong friendships to save one dime of the value of their property–and you will be too if you ever buy a house.

So, if your house is in a residential area, what can you do to preserve and enhance property values and the feeling of safety in the area? For example, can you help people with their yard and gutter work or help keep the local park clean? Can you help with the community watch? If you find ways to give them what they want, the neighbors may even cut you a little slack from time to time when things get boisterous at the House.

Finally, don't forget your teachers. All things considered, faculty would rather students show up for class, be prepared, ask interesting questions and do well on tests. Can you make sure your members give them these things? Wouldn't these be good things for any student to do? Later, perhaps, you could ask your favorite finance professor to come in and talk with your members about how to start managing their money when they graduate. Maybe that cool communications instructor will help you produce a recruiting video.

The **FAME** process provides a good way to approach this:

- **F**igure out who the target market is—the stakeholders.
- **A**cknowledge the problem(s) they face – what they want, what they are looking for.
- **M**ake a role for yourself in solving that problem.
- **E**xplain the solution you propose.

Then do it.

By the way, if this sounds like it relates to the discussion on branding, you are correct. But it goes beyond that. It's also about being a positive influence on our communities, about being important organizations whose contributions would be missed if they were gone.

Even an organization that is firing on all cylinders cannot remain the same. If for no other reason than the turnover of membership, the organization will change. Indeed, it must change because the environment will never stay the same. You might as well go ahead and plan for it.

▶

CHANGE

Plan to change something every year

Run the annual planning meeting as if the organization were being built from scratch for the current environment.

As the environment changes, you and your chapter have to be willing to change to adapt. In the long run, *everything* can be changed. There is no practice or tradition that you have to keep at the expense of the survival of the organization.

So, when you sit down at the annual planning meeting, put everything about your organization on the table when it comes to making sure that you are well positioned to thrive. Then pick two or three things to change that will help you adapt the most.

While you are at it, make sure that it is part of the chapter *culture* that people expect the organization to change to keep up with the changing environment. Bring up what's happening in the wider world in chapter meetings as points of information so that members understand that the world outside their doors is marching on with or without them. That is also good preparation for doing business in an uncertain world.

Don't fear breaking a few eggs from time to time

It costs to change an organization and it can be scary. A part of your usual pool of recruits may no longer be interested in membership. Members may have a hard time recruiting in a new (larger, you hope) pool. Maybe they have a poor record of accomplishment in terms of the new set of qualities the chapter is looking for. Your chapter might have a reputation to overcome. You might have trouble creating the policies and procedures needed to change, and some of your members may grumble about "going inactive".

But if the chapter needs to change, why don't members do what they should to help it change? Because…

Your members already have the chapter they prefer.

You might think that's crazy. Who would prefer a small chapter with no money, low grades, losing teams and a poor reputation? Yours, maybe.

Your members' choices have created the chapter you have

Your members already have the chapter they prefer.

The current state of your chapter depends almost totally on the effects of choices your members have made. Often, they are unaware of those effects. For example, members may rally around a group of guys who cannot or will not pay their bills. They do this thinking they are endorsing brotherhood but the *effect* is that dues are optional if you're popular. People think, "If that guy gets a break, why not me or my friend?" The ultimate outcome of this path is cash flow problems. *Your members prefer a chapter with cash flow problems to a chapter that holds people accountable for paying their bills.*

Members may look around at a meeting and be happy with the guys they see, so they choose not to help out with recruiting. After all, they've gotten the friendships they joined for. They are choosing therefore not to continue the organization. They choose not to hand it on to the next generation as it was handed on to them. *Your members prefer a chapter that will die soon after they leave to a chapter in which they take responsibility for recruiting.*

Members may think they are doing their slack friends a favor by insisting that a person may make up for deficiencies in one area of standards by excelling in another. "Yeah, we all know he's not serious about school but he's a fantastic rusher and we need to honor that unique contribution." The effect is that members can choose to be unaccountable in any number of standards areas as long as they "make up for them" in others. Unfortunately, the decision about whether a person is "a good member overall" will eventually degenerate into a popularity contest. When that unpleasant truth is pointed out, the chapter will lower its standards to make sure that everyone qualifies as a good member overall. It won't be called lowering, however, it will be called making standards more "realistic". *Your members really prefer a chapter with no standards to a chapter with standards.*

No matter the situation of your chapter, members have adapted to it. Change also means uncertainty to your members and many of them would rather deal with "the devil they know" than the one they don't.

What can you do about this? At least, you can point out the consequences of their choices to members. They won't like it but it will be an eye-opener to some at least. It won't make insisting on changes easy but making people realize the long-term consequences will lead some of them to think more carefully about the messages their choices send to other members.

Be aware of the many ways members can prevent change

Since organizations can change only if individual attitudes and behaviors change, many members will resist efforts to change the chapter either by denying that there is a problem or by watering down the proposed changes so much that they don't have to change anything about their own behaviors. You can propose the most logical set of measures in the world and people will still oppose it if they think it will require that they and their friends do a single thing differently.

A particularly destructive tactic is to "address the issue" by creating an extensive and complicated system of by-laws and procedures that looks wonderful on paper but that is too much trouble to actually enforce. This is the worst for the chapter because it allows the organization and other stakeholders such as alumni and the administration to claim to have addressed a situation when, in fact, they have only passed a by-law that will not be enforced when it bumps up against reality.

Members can also passively resist change by calling for more and more talk about an issue or simply refusing to do the work of change. They may not show up for meetings at which things were discussed, using homework or other meetings as an excuse, and then claim that no vote should be held until "everyone has had a chance to be heard." They may try to prevent a quorum from being present for votes. And, finally, if they are in positions of responsibility, they may simply not fulfill their duties, counting on the usual lax accountability for officers to protect them. They may even run for offices or committee positions in which they plan to do nothing.

The point is, as bad as things might be, expect that some of your members would rather things stay that way than have to change anything about themselves or their behavior. Count on it and know that there is no good way around it—no matter what you do, a few people will claim to have been cheated, that brotherhood has gone out the window, that (with tears in their eyes) they would not have gotten a bid or been a member for long with these new standards, etc. But also remember that they believe that it costs them *nothing* to oppose change whereas having to comply with changes may cost them a lot.

When change comes anyway

Some members may find that different emphases and standards lessens or eliminates the benefits they used to enjoy. In the best case, these members will avoid behaving in ways that work against the new emphases and will hang on until they graduate.

However, some people simply will not get with the program. They will say that it would not be fair to insist that they and their friends change since they joined under the old standard. That puts the chapter in the confusing and difficult situation of considering dual standards—one for new members and another for those "grandfathered" in.

Dual standards are hard to pull off well because new members will take their behavior cues from older members. This makes turning around the culture of the organization more difficult, drawing it out when the organization needs to demonstrate competence in the new way.

As painful at it can be, the best course is to hold everyone to the same standard and let the chips fall where they may. Phasing some changes in is an option as long as they are phased in for *everybody*. That might persuade some older members to remain. But you would have to be frank with the new guys about what changes are other coming up and emphasize that everyone will be held to a single standard.

Keep moving forward

The fraternity does not owe any senior the experience he had in mind as a freshman.

Environments change and organizations that want to remain successful must adapt. A given niche may shrink over time and, occasionally, the chapter might need to identify groups that are more promising or diversify. This can be painful.

Occasionally I have heard an upperclassman stand up and with a tear in his eye proclaim that, "If I walked up to this place today, I doubt I could get a bid. I might not even want one." My response is, "Relax. You've already got your bid and we're not taking it back."

Organizations must evolve to survive and the standard is set by current and future circumstances and needs, not by the past.

Consider how companies phase out old products and introduce new ones each year even though that usually means retraining or even laying off thousands of workers. What are the consequences for companies that fail to adapt?

Consider how many professions, such as medicine and accounting, require that their members have a certain number of continuing education hours each year to remain certified as the state of technology changes. What are the consequences for people who fail to keep their certification? If credentialing bodies did not require continuing education, what would be the consequences for customers of those doctors or accountants?

Consider how the best colleges and universities raise their admissions standards each year or change their curricula to adapt to the changing business and social environment. What effect does it have on the value of a degree from that college or university if it fails to adapt? I have degrees from Georgia Tech and, every year that I hear the admissions bar has been raised, I'm happy because the degrees I hold just became a little more valuable.

I've heard upperclassmen complain, "This is not the same place it was when I pledged." My response is, "I hope not. Our membership turns over completely every few years. It'd be mighty strange if we didn't change. Besides, if we're not changing to adapt, we're dying." In fact, it might be a good idea to head off the disappointment earlier by mentioning to candidates, "Hey this place is going to change a lot over the next few years and you'll have a voice in deciding what direction it takes."

The world changes and it waits for no one. In business, no one is owed the job he was hired to do for as long as he wants to keep it. If the needs of the business change, the employee must change as well or find another job. So it is with a fraternity.

As in business, the chapter's need to survive is more important than the preferences of any individual member(s) to have an organization that appeals to them. Realizing this can be painful but it is necessary if an organization is to be free to adapt to the changing environment. This is powerful preparation for the larger world.

The pain is not permanent

It is painful the first time the chapter tells someone he is no longer a member or the first time a person or group leaves on their own because of changes. From a leadership and management perspective, making or letting this happen is a powerful statement about how serious you are about the organization.

It hurts, though, and it will never not hurt. Fortunately, most of the hurt is fear—fear of an unpleasant confrontation, fear of what other people will think, fear that your relationships with others may be affected, fear that you'll be accused of overreacting.

This is part of running a successful organization, however. For all the "wailing and gnashing of teeth" that goes on in the short run, the chapter gets over it and moves on, you get better at dealing with it. As Chuck Palahniuk points out in his novel *Fight Club*, "after a few fights, you're afraid a lot less."

Face the awkward

A colony or chapter must identify a niche and have a long-range plan for being the best on its campus in its niche. However, depending on how the environment is changing, your chapter may find itself realizing that the group, as the current members are happy with it, will not attract enough new members to make and keep the organization viable.

Sometimes, the current membership of the organization cannot or will not do the things necessary to make it more likely that the chapter will thrive. You may realize that, despite your liking for each other, together you possess neither the talent nor the resources to create something that will be competitive on your campus. Or your members themselves might realize that many of them really are in it just for hanging out with their friends and, therefore, are unwilling to put forth the effort to create an organization that has wider appeal.

The current membership may not be the future

If the people won't change then you have to change the people.

A chapter has only the resources that its members bring to it. If the chapter must change, either the members must change themselves or they must somehow recruit a lot of new members who are different from the current members in ways that benefit the organization--even if the current members are pushed to the side. You must not let a group of current members stand between the chapter and what it needs to become to thrive.

This sounds strange unless you think of the chapter as an organization like, for example, a coach must think of his team.

When the coach of an athletic team decides that he is going to change the direction of a program, the program direction is going to change. He would be faulted by everyone who cared about the team if he failed to make needed changes for the sake of keeping specific members of his coaching staff employed or specific players happy. Likewise, when a coach is prevented from making changes because his assistants or players have connections among the alumni or in the office of the athletic director or the president, the team suffers. That's a no-win situation for the coach, so people get on board or they get out or the coach finds a new job where he has a better environment for success.

Pressing reset

The charter belongs to the national organization, not to the local.

If a chapter is unable or unwilling to change in ways that represent the brand better on its campus, then the national organization has the right to revoke the charter and keep it until the current membership has graduated and the memory of them on campus has faded. In a business sense, it is nothing more than revoking the franchise agreement. While this might seem drastic to the members who are present when the chapter is closed, "pressing reset" is merely the first step in the journey to finding a new group to take up the cause on that campus.

Remember, the national organization is bigger than any of its members. It's bigger than any of its chapters. It can prosper in the end only by making sure that it is strongly and well represented on as many campuses as it can support. It owes its current and future members the very best it can do to make sure that *every* chapter is a credit to *each* chapter.

▶

AFTERWORD

I think that the college social fraternity is among the finest organizations ever created for enriching the lives of young people. We are uniquely positioned to foster friendships, teach life skills, and better our communities while having as much fun as one can have and not end up in prison.

We betray the intentions of our founders and willfully remaining ignorant of our nature if we try to make something strange and mysterious out of our organizations. We could be doing a better job honoring their legacies if we did a better job running our chapters.

In this book, I have provided ways of thinking about many of the challenges chapters face. Since, as a system, we have long used other ways of thinking to manage ourselves and gotten the results we see, these ideas and suggestions represent challenges to some organizations. Some ideas and suggestions will represent personal challenges to the opinions and practices of influential people in your chapter and among your alumni.

But, if your chapter is not where it needs to be, take some of the ideas and suggestions in this book and give them a shot.

Don't be caught in the crazy trap of doing the same thing you've always done but expecting things to turn out differently this time.

Challenge people who support the status quo to back up their ideas with more than appeals to tradition and platitudes of brotherhood.

If you ask someone what he proposes as a solution to a problem and he begins his explanation with "Traditionally, we've…" it's a sign that he hasn't taken the time to think about it. Call him out on the fact that he doesn't have a plan. Then get to work on one and try it out.

Don't let anyone get away with a statement that begins "Well, if people would just…" Instead, challenge them (and yourself) to think of why people *don't* do what you want them to do. Then think of how you could set things up so that their wants and needs are aligned with those of the chapter.

Above all, look around you at organizations of all kinds that accomplish the things they claim to be about. Examine them and see what you could apply to running your own organization.

It's not rocket science.
It's all out there.
Go get it.
Act on it.
▶

See Appendix A for suggestions of activities you can undertake to start implementing some of the ideas explained in this book.

APPENDICES

Appendix A: Activities

The Brand

Have a look at your website, your Facebook photographs, your t-shirts and your rush brochures, flyers or banners. From looking at your materials, would a person be able to tell what sought in a member?

Promoting Friendships

Make a list of the things your chapter does to promote the development of friendships by lowering barriers between members, helping them discover common interests, and creating trust among them. "Hanging out" and "going out to eat dinner together sometimes", are valuable but they don't measure up for an organization that is supposed to be about friendships. If yours is like most chapters, you'll have a short, maybe empty, list. If that's the case, send a message to headquarters and get a list of things you can do, starting with silly icebreakers and working your way up to the heavy stuff. If you find yourself uncomfortable leading these activities, ask an alumni volunteer or someone in the dean's office at your school to facilitate. If you are uncomfortable about participating at all, ask yourself what you are afraid of.

Develop to Strengthen the Organization

Make a list of the things your chapter does to promote the development of members into good followers and leaders, capable of competently running the organization. Do you do anything to help members develop their skills in areas that will help them be better members and more effective in their lives in general? For example:

- Time management

- Studying
- Money management
- Problem-solving and working in groups
- Thinking long-term, big picture

Does member development end with your "pledge program" as if you had enough time to do a good job training new members then? What does your candidate education emphasize—Greek alphabet, historical and symbolic trivia, simple memorization of officers' duties? If you shy away from helping members develop skills and abilities that will really benefit them and the organization, why is that?

Alumni

1. Sit down with or contact some alumni and ask them their impression of your chapter in the following areas.

   - Achievement in scholarship
   - Being involved in the school and community
   - Keeping social behavior under control
   - Staying out of trouble with the administration
   - Taking good care of the facilities
   - Financial stability
   - No hazing
   - The deportment of individual members, especially seniors
   - Having a membership from diverse backgrounds

   Do the same with the Greek dean at your school. Ask them to list the areas in which your chapter's performance would lead them *not* to recommend you to a sharp guy who would like to rush.

   Now, with this list, what are you going to improve? Pick one thing at a time if you have to but do not let this information go to waste. Document your improvements and let the alumni (and parents and the administration) know what you are doing.

2. Have a meeting with your advisory board and ask them what the long-term plan for the organization is. If there is none, propose to have the collegiate officers meet with them and create one. Let them know that you are committed to the plan and that they are empowered to keep the organization on track in the pursuit of it.

3. With your advisory board, discuss how well competently they are fulfilling the responsibilities of a board. If they are falling short, is there something you could do to empower them? Maybe they just need to know that you would like them to play that role.

4. If you do not have some kind of alumni organization, start one. It does not have to be official or big. You can start with a Facebook page, a LinkedIn page, and a blog that you post the latest alumni news on. All of these can be had free, by the way. In the end, alumni will probably have to run their own association but it is definitely in the interests of the collegiate chapter to see their alumni organized, so do not be shy about getting something started.

Competitive Environment

1. Get a handle on your competitive environment. Make a list of all the qualities that fraternities on your campus have that might matter to prospective members. Qualities might include academics, nice house, big house, athletics, community involvement, girls like them, specific demographics recruited, etc. Then classify each chapter on your campus in terms of each of those qualities. Use any scheme or scale you want. You should ask for the help of some objective third parties with this to keep your own biases

from influencing the classifications too much. With this list, identify areas in which there are so many strong competitors that trying to compete in that area now would probably be a waste. Identify areas where a large number of competitors are deficient. Those are area for targeting. Now, most important, come up with areas that are not on anybody's list. Are there things that prospects are or might be interested in that nobody is doing? Those are *prime* area for targeting.

2. Pick a few things that would make good differentiators that you can do well. You can add to the list later but starting by concentrating on developing some organizational competence and getting a few successes under your belt. Come up with ways that every member of the chapter will be expected to contribute to the chapter's success in these areas. Put them on the member rubric. No excuses. Everyone must play a tangible role in the chapter's success in these areas. This is how you are going to establish your chapter's identity on campus, and every member must live it.

3. Create a mission statement. With your alumni, create a description of an organization that you can all get behind. Then create a chapter performance rubric that you can use to see how close you are to walking your talk.

4. Publicize your successes in areas that you are using to define yourself. Get your name out there in whatever form will reach the intended audience—prospects, parents, administrator, etc.

5. Make sure all members know the fundamentals of time management, money management, and study skills. Engage in developmental activities that help members learn to function as part of a group as a follower and as a leader.

6. Draw the lines regarding membership à la carte along with participation in fraternity events. If you have been allowing

membership à la carte, there is no painless way to end the process but at least the pain will not last for long.

Breakeven Point

1. Compute your breakeven point in membership. If you do not have exact numbers, make your best guess. A spreadsheet would really help here.

2. Now that you know how big you need to be, take into account who is graduating or otherwise likely to leave in the coming year and figure out how many you need to recruit this year to replace them and still have enough members to operate above your breakeven point. Add a few to allow for unforeseen losses and you have a meaningful recruiting goal.

Privacy not Secrecy

1. Eliminate the need for secrecy. Create a list of all activities associated with your pledging, candidate, initiation and member development processes including all local rituals and even unofficial but common things that go on. For each of these activities, note what thing(s) you are trying to accomplish through them that are good for the fraternity.

2. Review the FIPG guidelines regarding hazing along with any fraternity, state, community or campus documentation that would apply to your situation. For each of your activities, note whether it is mentioned as prohibited in any of these documents. If you have doubts, ask someone from headquarters. If they know you are trying to make sure your activities are all within bounds, they will be happy to help.

3. "Light of Day" test. For each of your activities, note whether you would be content to have the entire campus know every detail about what you are doing. As a test of your seriousness,

put a descriptive list of your activities on your website and share it with the parents of your candidates.

4. Introduce transparency. Let candidates know that they are free to discuss what happens, in a general way, in any fraternity event with anyone. Especially mention the "serious" events or those in which people passed their limits in constructive ways. Ropes courses, for example. This can influence the public perception of the organization in ways that attract new members. Only insist that they respect other members by holding in confidence things said under the assumption of privacy. Ask them not to reduce the specialness of the ritual by discussing it in detail although they are encouraged to discuss it in a general way.

5. Make needed changes to activities that were formerly secret. Regarding activities that are now seen to be over the line or that will not stand the "light of day" test, note what you were trying to accomplish with those activities. There may be some worthy goals there. Can they be accomplished by beefing up other activities that are within bounds? Can you find other things to do that will pass muster? Ask other chapters, headquarters, and the alumni volunteers.

6. Get into the habit of openness. Invite non-members—friends, girlfriends, parents, non-member advisers, and others to show up for chapter events. Everything that is not ritual may be open. Done well, these events could make the chapter look good in the eyes of some important stakeholders.

7. Replace instead of remove—if you can. Keep in mind that, when it comes to membership practices, undergraduates are notoriously resistant to change even if the future of the organization depends on it. It is much easier to replace or modify an existing practice than it is simply to forbid it, especially if there was some good attached to it.

Influencing Behaviors

1. Whom would we like to influence and what would we like them to do? One could take hours to create a list but here are some common ones. We want...

   - Potential members who would strengthen our organization to select themselves into our recruiting process and those who would weaken our organization to go somewhere else before we have to deal with them.
   - Parents to gladly pay all or a large part of their son's membership expenses
   - Professors and leaders on campus to recommend us to people they think would fit well in our organization
   - Members to develop their money management, time management and study skills and save us a lot of problems as an organization
   - Members to pay their bills in full at the beginning of the term or in installments that ensure the chapter always has cash
   - All members to share in the work of running the chapter — no 80/20 for us. 100% participation!
   - Members to respect the fraternity's facilities and other property
   - Members to handle alcohol responsibly
   - Initiates to remain members, that is, paying dues and participating until they graduate
   - Sororities (the ones we like) to want to have mixers with us and hang out with us in general
   - The dean to cut us some slack when we screw up from time to time (which we will)
   - Our alumni to give us money, refer qualified prospects to us, show up at some chapter events, and help us with internships and permanent employment

   Taking the first group or person on the list, what could we do to influence desirable prospects to select themselves into our recruiting process? This is important since, for an organization that depends on new members, everything should be geared to maximizing the throughput of qualified prospects: identifying them, meeting them, convincing them, pledging them, and initiating them. So...

- What is in their interests? What do they like? Can we find some alignment with their interests and likes and ours?
- How can we put what we are in front of them so they are interested in us? Web site? E-mail? Campus event? How can we make it easy for them to figure out that we're a good match for them?
- How can we be easy to meet and get to know as individuals?
- If they come and see us, regardless of how it turns out, can we make them glad they did? Can we get them to tell their sharp friends about us?
- Can we help them see themselves as succeeding in our candidate and development processes? Can we make these processes obviously helpful to them?
- If they have questions, can we make it easy for them to get answers? Can we help them deal with their parents, if they have doubts?
- If the candidate or initiation fees are an issue, can we work out a plan that helps them?

Put yourself in the shoes of the people you want to influence and ask questions like these. Then execute. If this involves changing procedures, then do it. If this involves rethinking what you do as an organization, then do it. Become an influence machine. Reach out and affect your environment. Then take those skills and processes out into the wider world with you when you graduate.

2. Educate yourself.

- For some great insights into human behavior in a book that is surprisingly easy to read, have a look at "Influence: Science and Practice" by Robert B. Cialdini[22]. You could have an entire semester college course around this book.
- "How to Win Friends and Influence People" by Dale Carnegie[23] has been popular for decades for good reason.
- "Don't Shoot the Dog" by Karen Pryor[24] explains behavior training of dogs. However, everything she says applies to people as well. As with Cialdini's book, you could have an entire college course around this material.

Paths to Redemption

1. Do your by-laws give your officers a range of responses to offences by members or do they amount to either a slap on the wrist or bringing out the nukes with nothing in between? Create a set of appropriate intermediate level sanctions with the help of your Greek adviser, headquarters, and alumni volunteers that will pass muster in the bigger world but that will not be draconian. Create sanctions that make sense for the offences, are reasonable for college students to complete (not necessarily easy) and that can be easily monitored. This is much easier than trying to come up with something on the fly.

---

[22] Cialdini, R. B. (2001). *Influence: Science and practice.* Boston ; Toronto: Allyn and Bacon.
[23] Carnegie, D. (1936). *How to win friends and influence people.* New York: Simon and Schuster
[24] Pryor, K. (1999). *Don't shoot the dog!: The new art of teaching* and *training.* New York: Bantam Books.

2. Educate yourself.

   - Read "How Good People Make Tough Choices" by Rushworth M. Kidder[25] to understand the nature of ethical dilemmas and various paths through them.

   ▶

---

[25] Kidder, R. M. (2003). *How good people make tough choices: Resolving the dilemmas of ethical living.* New York: Harper.

Appendix B. Sample Dimensions of a Chapter Performance Rubric

These are presented as examples to generate discussion. Your chapter and board must agree to your own set of dimensions and measures depending on the mission of your organization and its culture.

Dimension	Satisfactory	Superior
bringing together men from diverse cultural and national backgrounds	• Percent of membership from groups traditionally underrepresented in the Greek system is at least 75% of their proportion of enrollment at the University.	• Percent of membership from groups traditionally underrepresented in the Greek system is equal to their proportion of enrollment at the University.
aiding new members to develop behaviors and skills that lead to academic success and requiring older members to demonstrate effectiveness	• All candidates demonstrate proficiency in note-taking, time management and study skills as a condition of initiation • Chapter enforces a minimum GPA standard for continuing membership.	• Chapter enforces a minimum GPA standard of good standing for continuing membership. • Each candidate and member contributes at least one standard file to the Chapter library
providing experiences to develop the leadership skills, moral and ethical sense and social aptitude of our members	• Chapter Development Program (DP) is implemented to the satisfaction of the Board. • 80% of chapter candidates and members advance according to schedule in the DP.	• 100% of chapter candidates and members advance according to schedule in the DP.

coordinating living and dining arrangements among our members	• Chapter officer maintains list of current living arrangements and moderates forum for coordinating future arrangements • Chapter officer coordinates dining arrangements at least once/week	• Chapter officer coordinates dining arrangements at least twice/week
creating social events and activities for our members and their friends	• Chapter hosts a semi-formal or formal event. • Chapter hosts an off-campus brotherhood retreat.	• Chapter hosts an off-campus brotherhood event beyond the retreat.
competing to win in sports and campus events	• Chapter competes in at least three competitive sports and places in the top three in its league in at least one	• Chapter competes in at least five competitive sports and places in the top three in its league in at least two
being involved individually with other campus and community organizations	• 80% of the membership logs participation in at least one other organization that is not partnered with the Chapter. • 80% of the membership logs at least 10 hours of community service with an organization that is not partnered with the Chapter.	• 100% of the membership logs participation in at least one other organization that is not partnered with the Chapter. • 100% of the membership logs at least 10 hours of community service with an organization that is not partnered with the Chapter.
partnering, as a group, with other	• Chapter logs a co-sponsored campus or	• Chapter logs or co-sponsors two

campus and community organizations	community service event with at least one other organization.	campus or community service events with at least two non-Greek organizations.
promoting mutually beneficial interaction among undergrads-alumni	• Chapter hosts at least one alumni event during the term and 50% of the undergraduates attend an alumni event.	• Chapter hosts at least two alumni event during the term and 75% of the undergraduates attend an alumni event.
acting to sustain our organization	• All members and candidates are on good academic standing. • All members pay their bills in accord with their payment plans. • The chapter has at least 20* members returning. • All items on chapter officer checklists are completed. • Chapter holds an off-campus strategic planning/recruiting retreat	• 50% of members and candidates are on the dean's list or higher honors. • 25% of members pay their entire bill at the beginning of the term. • The chapter has at least 25* members returning. • All items on chapter officer checklists are completed by the assigned officer. • Chapter holds a training day for new officers and interested members

* Depends on the breakeven analysis.

▶

Appendix C. Sample Membership Contribution and Performance Rubric

Generate a list of specific actions members can take to improve the chapter's performance by creating individual performance dimensions from chapter performance dimensions.

These are presented as examples to generate discussion. The chapter and board must agree to a set of dimensions and measures depending on the organization's chapter performance rubric. Ideally, measurements taken to evaluate Membership Contribution and Performance would overlap substantially with the reporting the chapter has to do anyway to its IFC and its HQ to document scholarship, leadership, service, etc. In that case, evaluating individual members would amount to little additional work.

Dimension	Satisfactory	Superior
aiding new members to develop behaviors and skills that lead to academic success and requiring older members to demonstrate effectiveness	• Contributes one standard course notes file to the Chapter library	• Contributes more than one standard course notes file to the Chapter library
providing experiences to develop the leadership skills, moral and ethical sense and social aptitude of our members	• Advances through DP in accord with schedule	• Advances through DP faster than scheduled
creating social events and activities for our members and their friends	• Participates in off-campus brotherhood retreat.	• Participate in at least two off-campus brotherhood events.
competing to win in sports and campus events	• Participates in at least one competitive team sport with the	• Participates in at least three competitive team sports

	chapter.	with the chapter.
being involved individually with other campus and community organizations	• Logs participation in at least one other organization that is not partnered with the Chapter.	• Logs participation with two other organizations that are not partnered with the Chapter.
being involved individually with other campus and community organizations	• Logs at least 10 hours of community service with an organization that is not partnered with the Chapter.	• Logs 20 hours of community service with an organization that is not partnered with the Chapter.
partnering, as a group, with other campus and community organizations	• Logs participation in a co-sponsored campus or community service event with at least one other organization.	• Logs participation in two co-sponsored campus or community service event with at least two non-Greek organizations.
promoting mutually beneficial interaction among undergraduates and alumni	• Attends at least one alumni event during the term.	• Attends at least two alumni events during the term
Academics	• In good standing	• On dean's list or higher
Finances	• Meets payment plan	• Pays entire term bill up front

Member Contribution and Performance Descriptions Based on the Rubric

- *Marginal:* More than three marks less than "satisfactory".
- *Participating:* No more than three marks less than "satisfactory".
- *Satisfactory:* No mark less than "satisfactory".
- *Superior:* No mark less than "satisfactory". At least three marks of "superior".
- *Exemplary:* No mark less than "satisfactory". At least six marks of "superior".

An option to rank order members by contribution and performance

If the chapter wants to (or must) be aggressive about improving the membership, you might take a technique similar to that used by Jack Welch, former head of General Electric[26]. Classify the members into three groups: superior, satisfactory and less than satisfactory. Then show the bottom group the door.

For example, on each dimension, score +3 for superior, 0 for satisfactory, and -2 for less than satisfactory. Sum the ratings for each member and rank them by the sums. The top 20% are eligible for honors. The bottom 10% are candidates for help or dismissal.

It might come across as severe in an undergraduate fraternity context but it will produce results. In a "cleaning house" situation, this would be as open and objective a method for getting on with the difficult work as one could create. If the

---

[26] Welch, J & Welch, S. (2005). *Winning.* New York: HarperCollins.

dimensions and measurements were made public, as they should be, and members were given appropriate time to adopt new behaviors, many members that you would ask to leave would probably self-select themselves out of the organization before you had to serve notice to them. Remember, we do not owe members unconditional acceptance. We owe them clear standards and fair appraisals.

▶▶